Dearest G
To my an;
loving "spir
loving , have
lee

May 21, 2010

MW01517079

A CALL
TO
GREATNESS

A CALL
TO
GREATNESS

The Exciting, Joyous Journey
Your Soul
Wants You to Take

by

CARRIE HART

Copyright © 2009 by Carrie Hart

All rights reserved. No part of this book may be reproduced or transmitted in any form or by any means, electronic or mechanical, including photocopying, recording, or by any information storage and retrieval system, without permission in writing from the publisher.

Published by Systematique, Inc.
www.Systematique.org

Published in the United States of America

To Valerie, for being at my side in this latest journey
To Mary, for being with me in so many before
&
To Ed, for always welcoming me home

Contents

INTRODUCTION

I woke up this morning before dawn with what has now become a familiar feeling: an urgency to get up immediately, come to the computer and write a book for you. It has come to me with such clarity and intensity that this is something I simply must do. A flow has built up inside me that wants to be made real, physical, tangible.

I know that I am to write a book for you that contains everything I have learned about spirituality since I began my journey in 1994. I am to sort through all of my explorations and experimentations and tell you only what I absolutely know to be true.

This means that I will set aside what I have merely read, yet never personally experienced. I will avoid the belief systems of religion and new age thinking, and speak only of what I know, without question, because I have seen it and felt it. And I will endeavor to present it to you in a way that cuts through all the theory and goes directly to the heart of the matter: what you can do to live a life of joy, love and peace. And, importantly, how you can open yourself to your own greatness.

For of those things I know with certainty, this is the most important and the most vital for you to understand and accept fully, deep within your heart: you have greatness within you. You, just you, exactly you, just as you are, with all that you have done and left undone, you are full of power and greatness.

This greatness within you has nothing to do with money or success as we define it in our society. It is largely irrelevant to the expression of your greatness how you make a living, whether you have a successful love relationship, whether you have children, whether you achieve financial security, and whether you are recognized and rewarded. You may well be very close to expressing your greatness and power right now, even though these other signs of success have eluded you.

You have a soul who has defined your life mission and has given you all of the power and talent you need to fulfill it. And this direction is at a very high level, like a personal North Star to follow, so that you may live your life in many different ways, yet still be heading in the direction your soul has laid out for you.

My goal in this book is to help you turn from distraction and toward your true direction, to step fully into the greatness and power that is within you. You may be surprised to find how simple it is to reach into your greatness and expand out from that and claim your vast power.

No matter how old you are, how much money or time you have to spare, if you have accomplished amazing things or apparently made mistake after mistake, if you have been a model of discipline or struggled constantly against yourself, the answer is the same: you have greatness within you, and this book is your call to find it and let it guide the rest of your life.

It is my wish that you may awaken each morning in love with life, facing the day with anticipation, enthusiasm and joy, ready to shine out with all that you truly are. Shine on!

THE TIME IN THE DESERT

My spiritual journey began as so many do, in a crumbling down of hopes and dreams, watching it all fall away and wondering what in the world to do next. Little did I realize at the time that what was crumbling was the wall blocking me from finding my way into the garden.

When you are in the desert, stumbling across the sand toward a distant oasis, it is difficult to realize that you could just as easily choose to live in an abundant garden, where the water of love flows endlessly and ripe golden pears drop into your outspread hand.

My mirage on the desert was a newly-obtained position as a Vice President, reporting directly to a dynamic woman who was one of the few female CEOs of the Fortune 500. Visiting her penthouse office on Park Avenue was like being called into the presence of the queen, and the courtiers fluttered and flustered around her, doing her bidding, all while she accepted calls from the rich and famous to arrange trips to the Hamptons. Between calls, she would drop a few instructions my way; three minutes of direct attention were my reward for the 5-hour red-eye flight from Los Angeles that she had asked me to take.

I could see why she had been featured in Fortune magazine—multiple times—as one of the 10 worst bosses ever, but I felt immune to it personally. True, she seemed to treat people poorly, but perhaps it was just as she said, that they just didn't work hard enough. She said I was different from the rest and that, through me, she could finally have the kind of person she deserved in her organization. But as another VP pointed out to me after I tied the employment knot, that was just the courtship followed by an all-too-brief honeymoon.

A year later, I had gained 30 pounds, but even that was not enough to protect me from the environment of fear we executives all lived in. She would schedule a meeting at 7 AM on Sunday, but not show until noon--and then scream at us until the veins on her forehead were bulging. She would ask us to work until 2 AM on a Friday night because her private jet wasn't cleared for takeoff until then. She would tell us to fly overnight to New York City and then refuse to see us when we arrived.

On the other hand, she paid us very, very well. So based on that, my husband and I went house-hunting. We walked into the house I now live in and it literally spoke to me. I was home. On the day of the move, I was immobilized with fear, fear that I would have to work for The Screamer for years and years, all to pay the mortgage. But move we did.

As it turned out, I needn't have been afraid, for my time with her was soon to be ended in a totally unforeseen way.

On my birthday in June, 1994, one friend gave me a journal and a book, *The Artist's Way* by Julia Cameron and Mark Bryan, and another friend gave me a book by Deepak Chopra. Both of these were unexpected, because I was about as skeptical and secular as one could possibly be. I had not been raised in any religion and had absolutely no interest in spiritual exploration. But as it turned out, I was about to need some spiritual help. I learned from another friend at this time that the HR Department at my company was interviewing job candidates in the evening—for my job! Apparently I was about to be let go.

And so it was.

What a devastating thing it was to be fired, even though I detested my boss and my job, even though it was literally making me sick with fear and dread. Still, it felt like a terrible rejection, especially for someone used to success in work.

As it happened, there was more crumbling to come. My husband became ill and was unable to work. Then my stepson's wedding plans fell through just after his college graduation, so he moved in for a time to lick his wounds and get a career going. And there we all were, sitting around in our big, beautiful, mortgage-laden house, unemployed, rejected and dejected. Luckily I had a severance package and some stock options, and this, together with paying the

7

penalties for early withdrawal on our 401K, got us through somehow.

So I certainly had time to read the spiritual books I had been given, books I found surprisingly interesting. I didn't fully understand them, but there was something in them that resonated. I also took advantage of the time off to get back to the singing and songwriting I had set aside in my whirlwind days as a bi-coastal executive.

And gradually, in the coming year, I began to see the gates to a garden, there beyond the crumbled desert walls. The gates swung open just a bit and invited me to enter. I could hear the running water and the song of the birds, could smell the perfume of the roses. And finally, well, I just walked right in.

THE GARDEN
BECKONS

There are many entrances to the garden of spirit, many different gates you may enter. I realize in retrospect that music was my early preparation, since that was the way I naturally experienced grace, either through the mysterious creative flow of a song that seemed to come to me from somewhere outside of myself or the feeling of having chills when I would deeply connect while I sang before an audience.

My most direct entrance into the garden, however, was through the conscious training and use of intuitive senses, something I explored for the first time in 1995.

One day that fall, my husband and I went to a bookstore, a favorite thing to do. But when we pulled into the parking lot, I found myself saying that I would just wait in the car while he went in and got a book for himself. It was as if I knew my life was about to be changed and I wasn't at all certain I wanted to go along with some unknown program.

But I quickly came to my senses, laughed and thought, "That's ridiculous, I love bookstores," and walked in. Once in, I felt oddly compelled to walk to the aisle I never, ever visited, the one that had religion and spirituality. I went over to the New Age section, pulled a book off the shelf called *You are Psychic*, by Pete Sanford, sat right down on the bookstore floor and began to read.

When my husband finally came to get me, I was so embarrassed to be reading such a book, that I put it back on the shelf. Then I thought, "That's ridiculous, the book was really interesting," so I bought it, but I did tuck it under some 'normal' books so that no one would notice.

When I got home, I just devoured the book in one sitting. I tried out all the exercises and well, the rest is history.

YOU ARE INTUITIVE

Before I continue with my own story, I need to stop here and talk about so-called psychic phenomena. I have chosen to use the word 'intuitive' instead of 'psychic' because there is so much associated with the word 'psychic' that is not what I mean at all.

Anything that seems dark and forbidding, that makes you feel afraid or that can only occur secretly in a dark room, is not what I mean. The intuitive senses as I know them are bright as sunshine, accessible to everyone, transparent and open. And they are quite simply a natural and easy part of our everyday lives

I believe this topic is very important, not because the use of your intuition is in itself a spiritual experience, but because it can help you lead a healthy, fulfilling life, one in which things seem to flow more easily. And also because it can, as it did for me, give you tools to lead you into spirituality, if that is your path.

In the Wizard of Oz, there is a good witch, all beautiful, light and glowing, and a bad witch, dark and ugly and mean. If there is a bad witch, a dark side, to all of this, I have not experienced it. I have chosen the good witch only and I recommend you do so as well. If you read or experience something that makes you fearful or just doesn't feel right, then just say no.

Well, I will tell you about one experience I had that might have been a touch of the bad witch—but since I turned away from it, I really can't say. And I tell you about it only because it demonstrates that you have the choice, always, to stay within light and love.

I was very frustrated that my middle-aged fingers just couldn't seem to learn to play the piano well. In this state of frustration, I was walking in my garden, when the voice of a black man with a Southern drawl came into my mind. He introduced himself as Casper, the Blues Man, and said he would be delighted to show me how to play the piano. But before I could even respond, my good friend Quado (more on him to come) was right there in my mind, saying in no uncertain terms that I was to send Casper away. So I did. And that was that, my only possible brush with the dark side.

I have no idea what would have happened if I had not told Casper to go away, but I do know that I still can't really play the piano!

But now to the important part, your intuitive senses. From my years of exploration and experimentation, here is what I know to be true.

- Your intuitive senses are just as natural as your other senses of taste, feel, hearing, smell and sight. You were born with them. You were probably taught that they are not real, and so you learned to ignore them. But they are there. They are not paranormal; they are absolutely normal.
- As with your physical senses, everyone is unique in their natural abilities. You probably have most of the intuitive senses to some extent, but some may be like having 20/20 vision and some may be fuzzy and unclear. If you experiment and find that one intuitive sense doesn't work well for you, just try another. Then practice using the intuitive senses that come most naturally and easily to you.

Following are the intuitive senses that I am personally aware of. There are probably more, but this is what I know.

Knowing

Knowing is that really quick flash that comes and goes, like when you suddenly know your sister is on the other end of the ringing phone, even though you haven't spoken to her in months. Or you suddenly know you need to go check on the baby, right now! Without realizing it, I had been using this ability quite a lot in my work in computers, where I would suddenly just know where to look to find the answer, thus bypassing hours of analytical drudgery.

I have also been on the receiving end of Knowing. That Screamer I worked for had an uncanny ability to look at a page full of numbers and be able to ask about the one entry you couldn't justify or explain. She just knew.

I am not sure that this sense can be enhanced beyond its natural presence, but you can certainly enhance your awareness and response to it. We have all had the experience, some of us many times over, that we know something, but yet ignore our knowing. That's when we hit our foreheads in frustration and say, "I *knew* I shouldn't have done that!" Sometimes it was something minor — and sometimes it was a major mistake or opportunity missed. Either way, you will greatly advance your way in life, if you begin to listen to those hunches.

An important note here: Fear, worry and doubt often yell in your mind, but intuition usually whispers. Sometimes an intuitive knowing hits you full force, but most often not. Usually it is just a little tiny voice, and you need to learn to hear it underneath the other noise.

Feeling

The intuitive sense of feeling is often centered in your solar plexus, though you may also feel it in many places in your body. You know this sense well; you experience it when you walk into a room and people are just sitting there, but you feel that something is not what it seems. Perhaps you feel their conflict, because they have just had an argument. Perhaps you feel their attraction to each other, because they have just secretly kissed. But it's there, this feeling, tangible and often very strong, conveying to you the undercurrent of emotions not openly expressed. And

14

it may stay in the room, this feeling, even when the people are gone.

I think this sense explains what we mean when we say someone is phony. We see and hear what they wish to project, but our intuitive sense of feeling isn't buying it.

This is also that famous 'gut feeling' that people use in making decisions. It just feels right to go this way and not that. That feeling of rightness is a great gift, like an internal compass you can use to guide you through life. When you pay attention and act on this feeling, it may lead you to wonderful opportunities and new people, just because you felt you should turn right instead of left one day.

If you are extremely sensitive to intuitive feeling, you may find yourself easily swayed by others and sometimes confused about what you truly feel and what is coming from others. Again, awareness is your friend, for if you experiment and pay attention, you can learn to discern what belongs to you and what belongs to them, so that you can stand within your own truth and not be unduly influenced.

The very sensitive feeler can also be overwhelmed by others' anger, frustration or unhappiness. If this happens to you and you cannot simply leave the room, it may help you to put a physical barrier between you and the source of the harmful emotion, like folded arms, a desk, or simply more distance. You are feeling the physical energy of the other person's emotions, so treat it like something physical that can be blocked.

I believe this is often why people struggle with their weight. I do not think it is a coincidence that I gained thirty pounds in one year while working for a Screamer. Quitting my job would have been a healthier response, but I understand why I felt that I just couldn't eat enough: I was building a physical barrier to protect myself from attack. And when is the one time I don't have to worry about my weight at all, when it just seems to melt away? When I am falling in love and I don't want any barriers at all.

Hearing

Hearing may be a very strong intuitive sense in people who think in words, but there is a built-in paradox. The very people strong in intuitive hearing are also the people who disbelieve it, for it sounds so much like their thinking. They have unknowingly been using intuitive hearing all their lives, having internal discussions with their intuition as part of a natural problem-solving ability.

When I first read *You are Psychic*, I followed the exercise of asking for a word for a day. It's a very simple technique that will work easily for you if you are naturally strong in intuitive hearing.

1. Each morning, sit in a quiet spot with pencil and paper at hand.
2. Get into your relaxed, receptive state. With practice, this will be very easy to just slip into with one breath. At first, you may need a technique. What worked for me was to breathe deeply, slowly counting down from ten to one: breathe in ten, breathe out ten,

breathe in nine, breathe out nine, and so on down to one. When you reach one, you are at peace—if not, start over at ten!

3. It may help your intuitive hearing to gently focus your attention just in front of and slightly higher than the openings of your ears. But this is not necessary, so don't do it if it is distracting.

4. Then ask for a word for the day.

5. A word will just pop into your mind. Write down the very first word that comes to you, before you start editing and questioning.

Practice this very simple exercise each day and you will be amazed at the wisdom of that one word or phrase. It is also an excellent way to begin expanding upon this intuitive sense. After you have success with the daily word, then begin asking questions and writing down the answers. My favorite question is this: How shall I handle this person/situation? The open-ended nature of the question allows you to receive guidance that you would never even have thought to ask for.

Here's my favorite personal example. Shortly after I began consciously using my intuitive hearing, I was about to begin a new job and I had one opportunity to ask questions of the woman I was replacing. Before meeting with her, I asked my question: How shall I approach her? The answer came, loud, clear and very surprising: "Don't let her get away with anything!"

I was therefore surprised when I met her and found her to be perfectly charming and very helpful.

Then we began to go over the project plan for the project I was supposed to complete in a few months. It had all the right tasks and dates, but the detail wasn't there to support it. She tried to go past it very quickly and was dismissive when I asked a few questions. Then I remembered the guidance: "Don't let her get away with anything!" So I pushed and probed and wouldn't let her gloss over her plan, only to discover that the project was in trouble and that the dates she had promised—and for which I was about to take responsibility—could not possibly be met.

This early warning not only saved me and my team from failure, it also launched a seven-year career with that company, leading me to one of my more poetic examples of Word for the Day.

One day at dawn, the word that popped into my mind was "Compassion." This was an odd word to receive, for that very day I was expecting to hear whether I would be offered a promotion to Vice President at this very same company. But sometimes a word doesn't reveal its meaning until later,, so I just jotted it down, got dressed and drove to work.

Later that day, as I sat in my office waiting for the phone to ring, a great wash of gold light suddenly went across my inner vision and I knew the job was mine. I was summoned into the office of the Senior Vice President, the woman to whom I would now be reporting. On her desk was a rock with the word "Compassion" carved upon it.

If intuitive hearing is one of your strong senses, I urge you to make use of it at every occasion, whenever you have a decision to make, whenever you are walking into a new situation with people you do not know, whenever you have a difficult situation to resolve. Just leave the question open and capture the first response. Just ask: How shall I handle this?

This book is a direct result of that practice. This morning I asked: "How shall I focus my day?" And the answer came, loud and clear: "Write your book!" So here I am.

By the way, this question also works for people who are stronger in other senses; they may simply get the response in a different way. Rather than words, some people would see a picture, or have a feeling or a knowing. However it works for you, do it—a lot!

One last word on intuitive hearing. It is this sense that led me to Quado, who then led me to everything else this book is about. But Quado is such a big topic in my life, that we will reserve an entire chapter for the telling of that adventure.

Yet one more word. For me, intuitive hearing is something that happens inside my mind. It is not an external voice. This internal voice sounds like my own thinking, but it has a different feel. That, plus it tends to be located in the center of my mind, not on the right or left. It took me some experimentation until I could truly discern my own thinking from my intuitive voice, and I am always susceptible to some overlap. That's why it is so important to capture the very first words that pop into my mind, before my mind tries to take over with the tired old thoughts I am trying to reach beyond.

Seeing Energy

I suspect that there are many forms of intuitive seeing, but I have broken it out into the two I have personally experienced: Seeing Energy and Seeing Visions.

Here is one exercise of Seeing Energy that most people can do.

1. Stand somewhere inside where the light is gentle and not too strong.
2. Stand in front of a wall of a light solid color. A white wall in dim lighting is perfect.
3. Hold your two hands up about six inches in front of your eyes.
4. Extend your index fingers and touch them together
5. Let your eyes relax and unfocus slightly
6. Now slowly move your index fingers apart and see how they remain connected by a glow of energy
7. Then just play with the energy, watching it contract and stretch as you move your fingers.

There is nothing particularly intuitive about this exercise; it is simply demonstrating that it is possible to see energy. And this is important knowledge to have if you wish to see auras, which can, in fact, be a great intuitive tool — or so they say.

I will not spend much time here on auras, simply because they are not my strength. When I practice, I can see them in ideal conditions. When I practice a lot, I can sometimes see one or two colors within them. But it has never been more than a parlor game with me. Since I am much stronger in other senses, I have chosen to leave this one alone.

I will tell you what I did learn about the ideal conditions for viewing auras, at least for someone like me, who needs ideal conditions. Have a friend sit in dim light against a white wall. Just ask them to close their eyes, breathe calmly and be as relaxed and centered as possible.

Look above them and slightly off to one side. Then unfocus your eyes. You may see a glow around their head in your peripheral vision. But if you look directly at them, the glow may disappear. It feels odd, but you will see the energy best if you allow it to be seen in peripheral vision.

But I must leave this for you to explore through the many books written on the topics of auras and the entire field of healing based on an ability to see and understand energies in the body. I believe it to be real, but simply lack the depth of this gift.

I did have one interesting experience with seeing energy that I can share. I pulled into a mall parking lot and pulled out my car keys. I had a fleeting vision of a bar of green energy across the ignition key, on the plastic part at the top. I didn't understand what I was seeing, so I chose to ignore it and went shopping. When I returned and pulled out my keys, I saw that my car key was missing; it had broken off right where I had seen that glow. Luckily I found the key lying on the ground near my car.

Seeing Visions
Seeing visions and visualization are close cousins, related, but not quite the same.

21

Visualization is what happens in your mind when someone says, "Picture this." My sister cannot visualize at all and I have had clients comment that it was not a strength of theirs. For me it is like a vivid color movie with a strong focus in the center and blurring out to the edges. I knew someone who could visualize very spatially, knowing exactly how the couch in the store would look against the wall at home. As my home attests, that is not a use I can make of it.

Intentional visualization can be very useful to help make the desired effect happen, as you often see athletes using it. Visualization during meditation often combines intentional visualization with a touch of vision.

But here is the difference: in a visualization, you tell your mind what to see. In a vision, your intuition shows you what it wants you to know—and you don't know what it will be until it shows up. In other words, visions provide you with intuitive information.

You can learn to invoke a vision as a means to get specific answers. You may request a vision to answer the question, "How shall I handle this situation/person?" You may use it to see what is happening in that moment somewhere else, sometimes known as remote viewing (I've done this, but it isn't a great gift of mine). I have a friend who can locate lost items; she asks and just sees them wherever they are: under the car seat or behind the bureau. You can also ask for a vision to show you what you are meant to do with your life in a larger sense, something I explore in a later chapter.

22

When you begin asking for visions, it may help to have a technique to follow. But be aware that the vision may come to you well before you have completed your steps, especially after you have done this multiple times.

1. Sit in a quiet spot with pencil and paper at hand.
2. Write down your question.
3. Get into your relaxed, receptive state by breathing deeply. If you are tense, try breathing deeply while counting down from ten to one.
4. Gently move your attention to the place between your eyes. Feel that space expanding out to the side, wider and wider.
5. Silently ask your question.
6. Observe the visual answer. Then write down a description of what you saw, along with any words or feelings.

In my case, when I speak of visions, I am speaking of something that appears within my mind, with or without my eyes closed. When I first began requesting visions, I noticed that an intuitive vision had a slightly different quality than an intentional visualization. It was somehow grainier. But that differentiation seems to have faded over the years, as my intuitive visions have become clearer and it has all begun blending within me.

Intuitive visions may also come unbidden. In another chapter of this book, I will tell you about a very important vision I had about our relationship to our souls. I will also tell you about a number of visions I had of Jesus.

I find intuitive seeing useful in many small ways as well. Sometimes a magazine or an article suddenly appears brighter to me, calling my attention to it. I have experimented successfully with writing my choices down and asking for the best choice to be brighter. I sometimes picture my choices as forks in a path through a forest, and ask for the best choice to appear brighter. I have also come to associate the color gold with a positive answer, as happened when I was waiting to hear about my promotion.

When you practice opening up your intuitive senses and then invite them to be a part of your life, you will begin to learn the many ways your intuition speaks to you, your own codes and signals.

<u>Bringing It All Together</u>

One of the wonderful uses I make of all this is during an intuitive adventure. This is something I do professionally, on my own or with intuitive colleagues, for individual clients or for groups.

I call it an intuitive adventure because I have no idea what will happen. I enter my meditative state, close my eyes and begin speaking of what comes to me, what I intuitively see, feel, know and hear as we journey. When I first began doing it, I was writing in longhand in my journal; then I graduated to typing it out on my computer as it came to me, and then finally to being able to speak it aloud as it came.

Much of this book will deal with what I have discovered on my various adventures, in the different forms that this has taken for me. I encourage you to accept your intuitive gifts with a great sense of fun, experimentation and adventure as well. Find a friend to practice with; it is great fun to just play.

For example, my friend Mary and I were playing with telepathy. I was picturing a candle and I asked her to tell me what she saw. She said she saw a microphone, so we thought our experiment had failed. Then I asked her to draw what she had seen. It was a long stick with something on the top, possibly a microphone, yes, but also possibly a flickering candle.

Hints and Warnings

Do not push. Intuition takes a light touch. I have had the experience many times where I was pushing for an answer and nothing sensible came until I gave up; then it just popped into my mind. It is rather like trying to remember a name; it will come to you when you stop pushing and trying so hard. And some of the very best things come when you are not trying at all.

Avoid trying to see into the future. After much experimentation, I have concluded that our futures are not fixed, and any attempt to see what lies in store for us simply results in confusion and misinformation. This is especially true when you push for an answer, because you are emotionally involved. If you feel desperate to get an answer, whatever you may get is highly suspect.

What you can do is ask what you should do now (as in "How shall I handle this situation/person?" or "How shall I focus my day today?"). The answer your intuition gives you is much more accurate than your logic and will lead you to the best possible future outcome, even though you are not privy to exactly what that might be.

Also, be aware that it is possible to misinterpret what you receive in your intuitive senses, as Mary and I did with the microphone and candle. You can mistake what you 'get' intuitively, just as you can mistake what you see or hear in the physical world. So before you make important decisions based on intuitive information, ask yourself if what you got truly resonates with you. Put the choice out there and verify it through several senses. Does it feel calm and settled in your solar plexus? Does it look bright and golden in your inner sight? Do you hear "Yes!" in your mind? Do you just *know* it is right?

And then ask the deeper questions that go beyond your intuitive senses: Does this choice come from love instead of fear? Does it ask you to open yourself to new ways of thinking and being, to evolve into greater wisdom and caring? Does it require deep courage of you? Does it challenge you to believe in yourself and your own wonder and greatness?

And if all of these answers are yes, then do it. Make the brave choice; take the courageous action. Do it even though it feels scary-good, that state where you are excited but scared, because you are expanding beyond boundaries and taking new risks, like stepping on the stage to sing for the very first time.

Why this Works

I really don't know why all this works; I only know that it does. I invite you to join me in learning to use these senses without needing to understand how it can possibly be true. Join me in the world of ambiguity and mystery, where the rules fade away and wisdom takes their place.

It is not necessary to have any particular belief system in order to benefit from what is there for you. It is not necessary to understand electricity in order to learn to turn on the lights so you can see at night. And it is not necessary to understand why intuition works in order to learn to turn it on at will and take advantage of the vast storehouse of information available to you.

Very specific guidance is available to us that seems to take many things into account: what others are doing and thinking; the likely outcome of events planned and underway; and our own desires for our future. The answers are all there if we will simply ask: What shall I do now?

THE END OF
SKEPTICAL CARRIE

I am going to step out of my chronology to tell you about a fairly recent event, something I consider to be a great accomplishment—and relief.

Through all of these years of spiritual exploration, I was also a very active skeptic. My sister even pointed out to me that I seemed to have two personalities: the 'normal' one she grew up with and the one who now talked to Quado, did spiritual healings, and so on.

Skeptical Carrie was really bothersome, because Spiritual Carrie would experience something wonderful, a deep vision or message of great wisdom, and then Skeptical Carrie would pop up saying "Balderdash! What nonsense!" and try to take the wonder away.

It was all right at the beginning, when I used to always start out saying "I know this sounds crazy, but let me tell you what just happened." But after a while, I didn't think it was crazy at all, but yet I just could not silence that tiresome skeptical voice. All I wanted to do was just relax and believe what I had found to be so true. But no, that voice would not leave me alone.

Finally, I decided I simply had to accept being two people: a spiritual explorer who traveled the universe making great and fun discoveries, and her companion, the endless skeptic, who never grew or learned anything and who doubted everything. It was just too exhausting to continue to struggle against her.

So I decided to write a book with both voices. Spiritual Carrie would speak, as she is speaking in this book, and then Skeptical Carrie would have a chance to pipe up and refute everything that was said.

I began the book, inviting both voices to speak. And the most amazing thing happened. Before I had finished a single page, Skeptical Carrie simply vanished. Once I gave up struggling and embraced her voice, she became silent.

It is always amazing to me to have a tangible, personal demonstration of a much-touted spiritual law. You know, sayings like "What you resist persists." And the advice to embrace and love all parts of yourself, even your illness. But there it was made into personal truth: when I embraced her voice and stopped resisting that skeptical part of myself, she just settled down into silence and allowed me to be in peace and speak my truth without doubt.

I thank Skeptical Carrie for her years of active service, when she made me question everything and taught me to rely on personal truth and experience above all. I thank her for insisting that I learn to live with ambiguity and mystery rather than accepting what doesn't quite make sense to me, and teaching me that "I don't know" is better than just repeating words that others say.

I thank her, too, for this book, for I could not have written it without her even more loving silence, when her many years of active service were over.

QUADO

I could not possibly write a book about intuition or spirituality without talking of Quado.

I must invite you again to join me in mystery here. I really do not know who Quado is. If you said he is simply an aspect of me, I could accept that. Or if you said he is an aspect of God or the Great All, that would be all right. Or if you wanted to fit him into the new age concept of a spiritual guide, that could work. And the Eastern concept of an Ascended Master would probably work for me as well, if only I understood what it meant.

All I know for certain is that there is a wise and loving voice I am privileged to hear within my mind. And I call him Quado.

There is a little stone bench in my garden, surrounded by a curving white azalea bush. As I sit on the bench, I can see my rose garden and then the tall Eucalyptus and pine trees beyond the hedge. It was my practice for many years to go to this garden just before sunrise, pen and journal in hand, to ask questions of my intuition and write down the answers I received. I would bundle up in a blanket and dip into the well of wisdom while listening to the birds greet the dawn.

I had graduated quickly from my Word for the Day exercise to asking more complex questions and receiving fairly long answers. These answers were coming to me from a source I referred to as My Angels, since it felt like multiple feminine voices. I was starting to have a lot of fun, asking questions for my girlfriends.

As an aside, I must say that it was some time before I had the nerve to tell my husband what I was doing—it still seemed so crazy to me. When I finally did confess that I was going down to the garden each day to talk to voices in my head, he took it in stride. After all, he's interested in abstract mathematics, and nothing is stranger than that!

One day, in November of 1995, as I was asking for guidance on behalf of a dear friend in trouble, the answer came in a new voice. The voice was still inside my own head, but it was strong and authoritative and had a masculine feel. And the answers were weighty and wise, taking me to a deeper level of understanding and certainly not at all the way I was used to thinking and approaching life.

Then I said, "Who is this?" and the answer came: "I am Quado." Quado and I have been talking ever since. (By the way, it is pronounced with a soft ah, as in KWAH-doe.)

In 1999, I began putting daily Quado messages out on the internet and over the years, thousands of readers have been kind enough to join me through many adventures of spirit, all led by Quado.

Incidentally, Quado has made it clear that he is not my personal property. If you choose to reach him yourself, to develop your own personal relationship and receive his guidance, he will be delighted. You will recognize him by a deeply loving feel, like a cozy blanket just out of the dryer that you can wrap around you. He is the father you always wanted, giving you gentle but wise guidance and loving you unconditionally, even when you choose not to follow his advice.

You will see what a Quado message is all about in the following chapter, "The Maui Papers," where Quado assists me in understanding the visions I am receiving. I also hope you will visit us on www.Quado.com to enjoy more as they continue to flow out from Quado, via me, to you.

Below are just a few Quado snippets from the thousands of messages I have posted over the years, just to give you a taste of Quado.

∞

If you are not being yourself, showing who you are in what you do and say, how will the people find you, who are looking for someone exactly like you?

∞

The antidote to fear is action. The antidote to doubt is belief. Fear is a bully. Doubt is his sidekick, telling you not to stand up to Fear. For both know that Fear has to back down when you look him in the eye.

∞

You are surrounded by love, guidance and helpful hands. But you need to know that the angels just love action. When you take a deep breath, face down your fears and commit to courageous action, the angels get to work on your behalf. You can hear them as they toss down their magazines, turn off the TV, fluff up their wings and say, "Well, at last she's going to do something about it. Let's get to work!"

∞

You are an avocado. On the outside is the skin, the part you present to the world. Just under that is the soft emotional part, formed from your childhood injuries and joys. When people go beneath their skin and discover this emotional self, they often think they have uncovered their true selves. But it is not so.

For underneath the emotions is the core, the center, the seed, and it is strong and resilient. It has the ability to create new life. This is your spirit, your soul, and it lives on long after the skin and the pulp are gone. Go here for guidance, for answers. Glow golden from this center and let it color all that you do and are.

∞

Life is like floating on an ever-moving river. If you face backwards, looking at the past, you may miss your chance to influence your future. Face forward, dip down your arm and use it like a tiller, sensing and using the natural flows to position yourself for that fork you see coming up. If you get caught in the rapids, go completely into the moment and rely on your intuition to help you dodge the rocks. And when you reach that nice flat spot after the rapids, just float on your back and gaze at the clouds for a time, enjoying each moment to the fullest.

∞

When you feel as if you are on a stormy sea, tossed by the waves, it is time to go deep. Come down under the waves and feel the peace, the silence. See how you grow gills and can learn to breathe down here. Allow your eyes to adjust to the light so that you can see the wonders that live in the quiet depths beneath the drama of life.

∞

You may choose to walk the road that others have laid out, long, dusty and crowded. Or you may move off a bit to the side, where it takes a little longer, but you get to walk or dance with your bare feet in the grass. Or you may take a deep breath and enter the mysterious forest that beckons beyond the grass. And inside the forest you might find such wonders that you are suddenly lifted and soaring, and you reach your destination in ways you do not even know exist.

∞

Readiness creates the energy of fulfillment. If you meet a record producer at a party tonight, will you be ready to sit down and play your song on the spot? Will you have your demo in your pocket to give her? Will you be looking and feeling great, ready to stand up and entertain? The angels know when you are ready for them to bring the right people into your life.

∞

Use your intuition to spot opportunity while it is still in the bud. The rose in the full bloom of summer is sought after by many, but the rose in the bud has a long blooming time ahead and will be glad of your company along the journey.

∞

People seek wish fulfillment and manifestation, the spiritual ability to bring something into being through intention. But ultimately, it is a paradox. For if you were so completely enlightened that you could manifest anything you cared to at any time you wished, you would have no desire to do so. For in that highly enlightened state, you would realize the perfection of everything exactly as it is.

∞

Rather than yearning for money, a fabulous career and the perfect mate so that you might finally be happy, why not just choose to be full of joy, peace, love and happiness right now, with everything exactly as it is?

∞

When you give yourself away to someone else, handing to them the responsibility for making you fulfilled and happy, then you will spend the rest of the relationship desperately trying to get yourself back. Learn to love others as an overflowing of love, coming from a deeply satisfied and complete center of love for yourself.

∞

You are like the snowflake, utterly unique in the world and one of a kind. But you are also the bank of snow, joined with all that is, connected so deeply that there is no separation at all. Both of these are true at one and the same time.

∞

You are a jewel of great value. If you are not shining now, it is simply because you have not yet removed all of the rock coating that hides you from the sun. If you are not sparkling, it is simply because you have not yet carved all of the facets that you might. But you are a jewel, and like the star sapphire, deep inside is the shining light that is you.

∞

When you feel caught and entangled, trapped in a web of troubles, remember that you are not only the fly, you are also the spider who wove the web. And this is the good news, for at any time, you may choose to stop the struggle and simply dissolve this web of your own making.

∞

Do not spend your time asking why: why something happened, why things are the way they are. No answer will be forthcoming, for the answers go beyond your ability to understand. Instead ask: How shall I handle this? What shall I do right now, in this moment?

YOUR MORNING
TIME

O ne of the most important things you can do for yourself is to set aside quiet time for yourself each morning, even if it means setting your alarm earlier and begging your family to work together to give you this gift. In fact, I believe it is imperative, the one thing you must do, every day, without fail.

For many years, I rose at 4 AM every day so that I could pour a full hour of loving attention out on myself before going to work. As it turns out, 4 AM is an amazingly wonderful time of day to be up, just you and the birds waiting to greet the dawn.

How I spend my morning time has varied through the years. I encourage you to allow your program to evolve as well. Just do the same thing every morning until you feel like doing something else, something centered in peace and a deep love for yourself. I have listed below the various programs I have followed, at least those that come to mind. Each of them was a great gift at the time.

Journaling

As I mentioned earlier, the gift of a book, *The Artist's Way*, and a journal, was instrumental on my spiritual path. The book instructs you to write in your journal every morning, just three pages, never lifting the pen and just writing whatever comes to you. I did this for many, many years and found it very powerful.

I cannot explain why or how it works, but for some reason, just dumping my mind out on the page every morning was a transformative experience. You may do as I did, which is to buy beautiful journals and great-feeling pens and make that beauty a part of the experience. But if that feels intimidating, as if it then demands more gorgeous writing than you believe you can produce, then just write on sheets of paper you toss in a drawer. It is the process that matters.

As you can imagine, my practice of journaling led very easily and naturally into my explorations of intuition. I could do my three pages, then ask for a word for the day, and then, when I became more intuitively proficient, ask for guidance. I have years and years of daily journals in which I captured Quado's advice.

Meditation

Meditating is such a wonderful gift to give yourself. It is truly transformational magic. When you meditate, everything calms down and falls into place. It teaches you to quiet your mind, so that you can hear intuition whisper. But most importantly, it teaches you to connect deeply with all that is, to reach a state of oneness.

There are many forms of meditation and many books written about how to meditate. I will explore here only those I have personally tried.

First, I must tell you that I have a very, very busy mind and I most often find lengthy meditation a bit trying. But somehow, even though I seem not to do it very well, when I have spent periods of time doing it anyway, it has a deeply transformative effect. Therefore, I encourage you to experiment and find something that works for you and then to do it every day for at least a month, perhaps a lifetime.

Recorded Visualizations

I have a number of meditations that were dictated to me by Quado and which I recorded. You may find, as I do, that using a recorded meditation or visualization is easiest, since it gives your mind something to do, a center to pull back to when your mind drifts. You just sit or lie down, close your eyes, follow the initial breathing exercises and then listen quietly for 20 minutes.

Mantra Meditation

Another method I tried is Deepak Chopra's Primordial Sound Meditation, which I understand to be a relative of Transcendental Meditation. You are given a personal mantra which represents the sound the universe was making at the time of your birth, based on some ancient formulas.

43

Then all you do is sit quietly with your eyes closed, breathe naturally, and repeat your mantra silently in your mind. When your mind drifts, you just gently bring it back to your mantra. Do this for 20 – 30 minutes. I put a kitchen timer under a pillow or in a drawer, so that I don't hear the ticking, just a quiet little ring when the time is up.

Sometimes I use a mantra that came to me: ohnta ah oom. You will read all about it in the chapter "17-21-35."

Moment Meditation
This is something I made up myself and try to do every day, all throughout the day, in addition to whatever my morning practice is at the time. It's something you can learn to do easily when you have become comfortable with the meditative state, a place of deep calm and connection.

Whenever I can, I take a deep breath and drop down into a meditative state. I do this gazing up into the sky while walking across a parking lot, pausing under a tree while walking along the sidewalk, gazing out a window at a tree while waiting for coffee to brew. Then I just feel myself expanding as I look at the sky or tree, feeling the oneness and beauty.

Other Meditations
I have also experimented with meditation simply by gazing at a beautiful object, and meditating by watching my breath as it travels in and out of my body. I once tried an exercise I read in a book, meditating by watching a little blue ball of light as it very slowly traced my body, traveling from the top of

my head, down the outside of my arms, between each finger, back up to my armpit, down my side, under my feet, between my legs and all the way around to the other side and back up to the top of my head, all paced to about 20 minutes for one cycle.. This last one drove me a little crazy, but that's just me.

Clearing

If you are going through a particularly difficult period in your life and are so full of anxiety or other emotions that you cannot even imagine sitting still for meditation, I recommend you do this energy clearing, followed by heartfelt affirmations.

In the following, because I am very visual, I emphasize what you see as well as what you feel. If you are not a strong visualizer, just go straight into the feeling and it will have the same effect.

Picture yourself on an open meadow, standing on the grass with bare feet. The sun is shining and little white clouds drift overhead. As you look up into the sky, little silver and gold particles of light begin to swirl around in a circle, around and around. This circle then forms into a cone of gently swirling light that begins to drift down toward you, still full of sparkling silver and gold. As it approaches you, you feel that it is full of love, warm and soothing, supportive and gently energizing.

Intuition

The cone of love and light now lowers to cover the top of your head and your eyes, and here it opens up and expands your intuitive senses, your natural sense of inner sight, inner hearing and that intuitive flash of knowing.

If this area seems small or restricted, then stay here for a while, allowing the energy to swirl and expand outward. Let it swirl and expand until it feels vast and open, until it is like gazing into the night sky, full of moving stars and planets, a great interconnected space. Take a deep breath as you feel your connection with everyone and everything that is, all accessible to you through your great intuitive powers.

The Quiet Mind
Next, the energy cone moves down and covers your entire head. Here, your goal is to reach peace and clarity, quieting the busy distractions that make it difficult to focus. Over time, you will find the right image or feeling to quiet down your mind. Here are a few that I have used:

- Picture your mind full of swirling dust, and then watch that dust settle, either just settling down naturally or washed down by a gentle rain.
- Picture your mind curled up like a cat on the hearth, letting the power of your mind blaze brightly while your thoughts quiet down for a nap.
- Picture your mind like a calm lake with a bird flying gently across; be the calm surface of the lake; be the bird.
- Picture your mind like a white board; erase all of the words and pictures until the white board is clear and blank.

If your mind is full of patterns and will not quiet down, just seek to lower the extraneous noise and allow your patterns to shine brightly; your goal is to find clarity and focus, if not silence.

Self-Expression
The energy cone now moves down to the throat. Let the cone of energy swirl here, opening up the flow of creativity and self-expression. See a flow of golden energy pouring out from your throat into the world, a flow that carries within it your talents, your wonder and truth, all of the gifts that you are here to share with the world. Let the energy swirl and swirl as it opens up this outward funnel wider and wider, until you feel that you are fully expressing who you are, shining out in your glory.

The Heart
The energy cone now moves down to the heart. As the cone opens your heart, allow the river of endless love to flow through. Know that the strength of the heart lies in being pliable and open. Let the flow of love melt any ice that has built up. Let it flow across any wounds and heal them. The more you allow the flow of giving and receiving to go through your heart, the stronger it will become.

If you feel that your heart is injured, that regret or blame has formed ice or that painful experiences have left wounds, invite a beautiful angel to appear before you. You may ask her to reach in and heal your heart with her hand. Or you may hand over the burdens of your heart to her, any heavy stones of unforgiveness and regret, and she will take them from you, then fly to the heavens and transmute them into love. Stand in quiet and gratitude as a gentle rain of love pours down upon you, washing you clean, filling you to the very top with sweet flowing love.

Solar Plexus

The energy cone now moves down to your center, your solar plexus. Within your center is a deep pool of water containing your personal truth. The water may be a little cloudy from old emotions: fears and worries, doubts, regrets, hurts. Let the energy swirl around and lift those old emotions away until the pool of water sparkles deep and clear.

If the energy cone is not enough to clear this away, if your center does not feel deep and clear and settled, then ask the angel to help you accomplish this. As with your heart, let her take all of your burdens from you and transmute them into love. Let her love then rain down upon you, clearing you and filling your center. Stay with her until your center sparkles clearly.

The Whole Body

Let the energy cone now extend slowly downward through your entire body, so that you are lit with the golden glowing energy of light and love from the top of your head to the tips of your toes.

Let the different energies combine and flow together. Let the truth from your center flow up and pick up love and courage in your heart and then move to your throat. Let your intuition flow down through your mind and to your throat. And now, combine them all, so that the self-expression flowing out of you combines and contains it all: your love, your truth, your intuition and your knowledge, so that you may find exactly the right words and actions to make yourself clearly understood by others.

Let the energy flow up and down your body. Let everything that is not light and love simply fall away. Let the angel help you achieve this state, if you wish. Become a bright glowing golden column of love and light.

Affirmations

Now, say the following statements aloud, feeling each one resonating in your body as you do so:

- Right now, in this moment, all is well. I have everything I need.
- Everything that I have done or left undone in the past has led me to now, this moment, and this moment is exactly as it should be.
- The past is gone and the future has not yet arrived; only this moment is real.
- I am deeply loved and held in the arms of a benevolent universe, guided and supported at every turn.
- I love and approve of myself and know that I deserve a life of love and joy.
- I own my world. My inner state of peace, joy and love creates my strong and healthy body, my beautiful surroundings and my loving relationships. It all comes from inside me.
- I create my own safety and security from the love and peace within me.
- I am love. I am peace. I am joy. I am.

49

Now you're ready to face the challenges of your life. Enjoy!

Conditioning

I have sometimes followed a conditioning program that I picked up from Gary deRodriguez, a Humanistic NLP practitioner, and then made into my own variation. It has worked well for me when I needed to move myself out of a state of confusion or fear and into focused action.

I know very little about NLP (NeuroLinguistic Programming), but one thing I recall is the theory that our conscious desires are not nearly as strong as the power of our subconscious mind, and that we are programming our subconscious mind every time we think or speak.

So if you tell your friends, "I have trouble controlling my weight," then your subconscious takes that as your truth and does everything it can to act on it, thus guaranteeing that you will indeed have trouble controlling your weight. If, on the other hand, you think and say: "I am slender, healthy and energetic," then that becomes the truth; that is programmed into your subconscious mind, underlying your choices throughout the day. In other words, think and speak what you wish to be true and avoid thinking and speaking of what you do not desire.

A very important part of this is to become what you desire emotionally, to put yourself in the emotional state that you believe you will feel when you have fulfilled your desires. By thus creating that state within you, you attract more of it to you. To paraphrase Wayne Dyer: You attract to you what you are, not what you desire. So this means that you must become it first. And that is what this conditioning program does.

Basically, here's the program, to be done every day without fail. It only takes a few minutes and it is surprisingly powerful.

For every change you wish to make in your life, make up a statement in the present tense. Hold yourself to no more than five statements; otherwise, this becomes too much work and therefore difficult to sustain. If you can do it in 1 – 3 statements, that would be even better.

I tend to keep my affirmations open-ended, like "I am slender, healthy and energetic," "I have the money to live as I choose," "My work is joyous and fulfilling," and "My home is beautiful, clean and orderly."

Some people believe that affirmations should be very specific, the exact weight you wish to weigh, the income you want, the career you are working toward. I really have no idea what is best, but I know for myself that the specific sometimes makes me uncomfortable, because I think that wonderful things can flow to me in so many different ways. But you should do whatever feels best to you. Also, feel free to start with one list and allow it to evolve over time, refining things as you go. The most important thing is just to do it.

Every morning, write down your affirmations with both your right hand and your left hand. That may sound odd, but it is important. After you write each one, picture yourself having achieved that state and feel the emotions of it deeply and clearly.

So, after I write "I am slender, healthy and energetic" with both my right and left hands, then I close my eyes and see myself joyously walking, dancing, trying on adorable, well-fitting clothes. I feel what it is like to pull on slender jeans and a T-shirt and go out in the world doing things with other people, feeling confident and vibrant.

Then go to the next affirmation and do the same thing.

After the affirmations, I write a little statement of what I am grateful for that morning, just to get me in the state of grace.

And lastly, I write a quick little essay on my life when all of my dreams have come true. In my case, it always begins, "I awaken in joy." Then it may go on to say things like, "Today is the dress rehearsal for my show at the Hollywood Bowl. I'll be working with so many wonderful musicians — it is so exciting!" And of course, I allow myself to fully experience the emotions of that life, a life I am truly living at that moment.

That's it. Short and sweet. And amazingly powerful if you simply do it, every morning without fail. And don't skip the part where you write with both hands. It is a bit difficult, but it is important.

All that's left to do then is to monitor your mind and your mouth throughout the day. When you talk, talk of the positive, wonderful things you are heading toward, not of your so-called problems or of the past. And if you catch yourself thinking in the old ways, just repeat your affirmations in your mind.

<u>Letting It Be</u>

Of course, the very best is when you are living in a state of grace, that flowing place where you accept everything just as it is and see yourself and your life through eyes of wonder and with a heart full of love and joy.

I wish for you many mornings in which you simply gaze at a tree in deep communion and peace, with no need to do or think anything at all.

RUNNING WOLF

After a few years of posting daily Quado messages on the internet, Quado and I had developed a following. One day, one of the Quado readers wrote to ask if I would do a spiritual healing for her. I was in the middle of responding to her that I simply wouldn't know how, when a shaman appeared in my mind to tell me that yes, of course we could do that.

This was my introduction to Running Wolf, a Native American medicine man who took me under his wing as an intern and worked with me on what turned out to be hundreds of spiritual healing sessions. As do most shamans, I worked with power animals, taking the energy and powers of the animals who chose to come with me and transferring them to my clients.

I received several wonderful blessings from the time I spent as a shaman, not least of which was concrete evidence of our interconnectedness. After doing this, I could never doubt the power of one

55

person's ability to see into the heart, soul and mind of another. It is simply truth.

I know this absolutely because I would work from a simple email request that often gave me no information whatsoever about the person requesting the healing. We had no contact on the telephone. I had no photographs. Just a name on an email. And yet, I would come up with exactly what they needed to help them through a difficult time.

I actually find it easier to do intuitive work in this 'blind' way, since I am guaranteed that what I receive is not edited by my busy and intrusive mind. I would take the emailed name and then go into my deep meditative space and ask for guidance. I would begin by going into a cave, dark and cool. There were usually Native Americans in the cave, gathered around a fire, chanting and drumming, including Running Wolf.

I would go through the cave to a deep, quiet pool of water. Then I would jump in the water and fall down and down, twisting and turning. Finally, I would tumble out into a green landscape.

Here, in the land of the power animals, I would walk across the landscape, which might be a jungle or might be the African plains. Or sometimes, it would be an ocean. I would journey out, looking at any animals that happened to appear, waiting for one to present itself to me. Sometimes the animal would appear right away; sometimes it would take a while. But eventually one would come and would present itself to me four times, from the front, back and both sides. I would then pull the power animal close to my heart and return to the cave.

I would find my client lying peacefully in the cave and would place the animal on or next to them. Then Running Wolf would perform a ceremony to join them and I would see them swirling around and around together, like a silver blur, until finally he said, "You are now one."

At this point, Quado would give me an interpretation of what powers this animal had given to the person. It was a very specific description of what they needed, and it turned out to be right on the mark. For example, one woman who received a songbird as a power animal had a deep suppressed desire to be a singer. Another woman, going through a difficult divorce, was joined by a rhinoceros who made a wide circle around her, protecting her.

After a time I expanded into soul retrievals. First I would retrieve the person's power animal, then the animal and I would go on a journey to find where they had a difficult experience and left a part of themselves behind. I would then bring those lost parts of them back to the cave, where Running Wolf would merge them together: the crying baby, the little lost child, the rebellious teenager, all now merged together and with the power animal, into one whole, centered and powerful person.

I found a boy cowering in the corner as his parents drank, grew louder and began to argue. I found a teenage girl floating up on the ceiling, disconnected from the woman she grew into. I found another woman in her kitchen, crying at the kitchen table as she discovered clues of her husband's infidelities. All of these Running Wolf and I joined back into the person who had requested the healing, along with a power animal who could help them move forward in strength and power.

And over and over, without having any prior knowledge of these people, my clients wrote to tell me that we were right on the mark.

And one day, this phase of my life was over. I built a website, www.PowerAnimalsUnleashed.com that allows people to use their own intuition to select a power animal so that they might do this for themselves. And as with Quado, Running Wolf is available to those of you who wish to become shaman healers. I know this, because he recently appeared in a Power Animals Unleashed Adventure I was conducting and invited a woman to be his apprentice. Just call him to you and let it all be as it will be.

But before we leave this time in my life, let me try to summarize what I learned, what I know is true and what I surmise, based on my personal experience:

- We are deeply interconnected, and when in a meditative-intuitive state, I can absolutely access personal information about people I have never met and know nothing about consciously

- When I do have some conscious knowledge of a situation before entering that altered state, I may get very direct and specific answers. When I do not, I will usually get things presented to me metaphorically. For example, in the case of the woman who always wanted to sing but had not, her power animal was a songbird and the Quado message for her urged her to follow her dreams. That she should sing was an obvious interpretation, but the message did not specifically say this; I learned about her singing desires later.

- Sometimes the most important information comes on very light steps. I once received a long message for a woman and at the very end, I got a flash: "She loves you." It seemed disconnected from the rest of the message and I had no idea what it meant, but I have learned to pass such things on. As it happened, this woman had just had a fight with her sister and this little flash meant more to her than all the rest.

- I think that what gets conveyed intuitively may be tied to the strong emotions of someone. What I read in people was normally related to the big, emotional experiences they were having, not the details of other things that did not truly matter. As I write this, I realize that this is probably the reason it is important for us to be in the emotional place of our desired life. Emotion apparently creates energy that flows out and has an energetic impact on the world.

- I had some experiences in that cave where a deceased loved-one appeared. Interestingly, they all had the same thing to say: I am at peace; I love you. They seem to be utterly detached from the emotional life they once led and no longer feel blame or regret. They were actually not at all interesting to talk to!

- I suspect that the power animals carry some tangible energy, going beyond their obvious use as metaphors, but I cannot say exactly what this is or how it could be. I personally do not subscribe to the shaman view of power animals as souls of actual animals who once lived; I think they represent a means to access energy of certain specific frequencies. But then again, metaphors are such powerful tools in the human mind, that it does not really matter. All that matters is that it works; power animals do heal. I encourage you to go to www.PowerAnimalsUnleashed.com and invite them into your life.

- I am pleased to accept Running Wolf as a mystery as well. I do not even try to theorize on him.

REIKI

Reiki was my first experience with physical healing energy. All of the work I did with Quado and Running Wolf was strictly mind, intuition and emotion. Reiki, on the other hand, is something you can feel physically. It is quite a mystery and just one more important step in my journey out of skepticism. For when I started experimenting with Reiki, I could not deny that something strange and mysterious was happening, something that was physically tangible.

Reiki is a Japanese hands-on healing modality. It is pronounced RAY-key and means Universal Energy. But it is not merely a technique you can learn from a book or video. It is passed from master to student energetically, via a ceremony called an attunement. After you receive an attunement, you can think the word 'Reiki,' put your hands on someone and they can feel healing heat coming off your hands. They may also sense an energy flow, but this seems to vary from person to person.

Reiki truly makes no logical sense at all. But yet it is physically tangible, easy to experience and requires no belief in anything whatsoever. I have absolutely no explanation for it, so I will simply share my experience.

My Reiki Experiences

First, I must say that I have not personally experienced any great miracles using Reiki. I am inclined to believe the stories others tell, but that has not been my experience. I have found Reiki very useful in healing bruises and cuts more quickly, in relaxing strained muscles, reducing pain in a variety of instances, including cramped muscles and headaches. If I had to guess, I would say that it increases the circulation, among other things.

On vacation, my teenaged grandson was surfing and crashed on some rocks. He came back to the boat and after everyone finished fussing over him, I gave him Reiki. He and I decided to experiment, so I applied Reiki only to the biggest cuts. We left some smaller ones untreated.

The next day, the areas I had treated with Reiki had no bruising and were healing nicely. The untreated areas, even though they had been smaller cuts originally, had swelling and bruising and were not as far along on the healing process.

I also had the experience of doing remote Reiki on my daughter; she called up and told me that her back suddenly felt as if it had a heating pad on it. But this physical response happened only once, even though I have done remote Reiki—successfully, I believe—many times.

History of Reiki

There was a Japanese medical doctor, Dr. Mikao Usui, who went to Mount Kurama in 1914 to meditate. No one knows what happened on Mount Kurama, but when Dr. Usui returned 21 days later, he had the gift of Reiki in his hands.

Dr. Usui opened clinics and practiced Reiki until his death in 1928. He initiated 16 Reiki masters, who were able to pass on the gift of Reiki. One of these masters passed the gift to Mrs. Takata, who brought it to Hawaii in 1938, and who was responsible for introducing it to the West.

Reiki Attunements

Western Usui Reiki is now generally taught in three steps, requiring three attunements. After the first attunement, the Reiki practitioner simply puts her hands on someone and thinks the word 'Reiki' to begin the flow of healing energy. For the second attunement, the Reiki student memorizes some symbols and uses these in subsequent practice. One of these is the symbol for remote Reiki, so that the healing can be done without physically touching. After the third attunement, the Reiki student is now a master, able to perform attunements and pass on the gift of Reiki to others.

I have also become a master of Karuna Reiki, something developed by William Rand and others. There are additional symbols associated with Karuna Reiki and I have found some of them particularly useful in applying Reiki to myself, to increase my learning capabilities and memory and to relieve my own aches and pains from time to time.

What I Learned

Reiki is taught with a lot of rules, at least in the West. Some of this requires you to memorize complicated symbols and trace them over the body being healed. After a time this was just too much effort, so I began just picturing them. Then that became too much trouble and I began just saying the word in my mind. There was no change in the Reiki power by simplifying the technique.

I suspect that all of the Reiki ceremonies and symbols serve primarily as a means to focus and direct intention and energy, and that the entire healing method could be simplified and streamlined. But then again, there is always a certain beauty and comfort to ceremony and symbolism, so perhaps it is best left alone. I merely suggest that if it bothers you as it is, it is likely open to a lot of change.

Reiki is a total mystery to me and I have no workable theories on how it could possibly be. But I have experienced it, so it became an important step along the road to the elimination of skepticism, one more instance of something I could not deny, because it is tangible, and yet have no system of belief to support it.

Homeopathy and Other Treatments

Along this line, I should mention homeopathy, just one more thing that makes no sense whatsoever, but seems to work. I won't go into it in any length, because I have only dipped into it lightly. It is very well known in Europe, but in the United States much less so.

Homeopathy involves energizing herbs through repeated shakings and dilutions, the power of the medicine actually increasing with each dilution. Not only that, but it uses the herb that, in full strength, would cause the very symptoms you are aiming to eliminate, somewhat similar to allergy treatments.

Homeopathy is a whole field of study, but everyone should at least have a tube of Arnica gel handy. Rub it on that pulled muscle, twisted ankle or crick in your neck and you will be amazed at what your body can do for itself overnight, given a little help.

My favorite book on homeopathy and other alternative medicine is *Radical Healing*, by Rudolph Ballentine, M.D. Ballentine explores all of the areas of medicine that our traditional Western medicine has denied, and demonstrates how best to use it all to excellent effect.

∞

As Shakespeare's Hamlet said: "There are more things in heaven and on earth than are dreamt of in your philosophy."

JESUS

My family did not go to church and I did not have a childhood relationship with Jesus. So you can imagine my surprise when he suddenly appeared in my life unbidden. I was not only surprised, I was frankly a bit dismayed. I had no desire to associate myself with, well, a lot of things.

But this Jesus was loving and tolerant, so after resisting for a time, I began to accept and honor his presence in my life. And so, I would like to tell you about my personal experiences with this extraordinary energetic presence.

My First Encounter

A few years after my first Reiki experience, I went to Glastonbury, England, to become an Usui Reiki master. After studying for a few days, we then went to Stonehenge for our master attunement. We were there after the park was closed and were allowed to enter into the circle of stones. The weather was blustery, with a wind blowing and big clouds drifting

67

across the darkening sky. I was one of about 20 people kneeling in a circle, our knees in the damp grass, our eyes closed, waiting for William Rand to get around to each of us and perform the attunement ceremony.

In my mind's eye, I suddenly saw that Jesus was weaving among us, wearing a white and blue robe, touching each of us on the shoulder and blessing us with love. When he reached me and touched my shoulder, I felt the most intense flood of love I have ever experienced.

I want to pause here and describe that moment, but I cannot find the words. Nor can I recreate it for myself, though I have tried, by inviting Jesus to revisit me again in that way. It was a moment of extreme grace, a moment in which my entire body experienced the deepest love imaginable—no, deeper than that—in a great flood that simply ran through me.

One friend who studies with an Indian guru said that I had experienced 'shaktipat.' I cannot say. I can only say that I feel deeply blessed to have known this touch of love, if only for a brief moment.

My Dream

Time passed with no more such experiences. Then, some months or years later, I had a dream. I was in a small town and everyone was all abuzz: Jesus is coming, Jesus is coming! They were looking everywhere for him and making great preparations, but he was nowhere to be seen. Finally, in disappointment, we all went home.

I walked into my humble little cottage and there he was, sitting in the kitchen, waiting for me. I asked him some question about the meaning of life and he answered me, but I couldn't grasp the words. I tried and tried, but I just couldn't understand what he was saying.

Then he went into a little room just off the kitchen where there was a cot. He told me he was going to lie down and that he would be there, sleeping, if I needed him.

And that was the dream. It ended with just the vision of him sleeping on a cot.

A Prayer

My next experience came when I was reading a book by William Rand about Reiki in July, 2007. Rand suggested that you call on an enlightened being for assistance during healing. He gave a list of suggestions and, not surprisingly, Jesus was among them. He seemed the obvious choice for me.

So I put out a prayer for guidance in healing and received an immediate reply, one that I would like to share with you now. The words I received from Jesus follow:

Before you perform a Reiki healing, invoke my presence with these words:

"Dear Jesus, I call you to me. May your loving presence surround me. May your healing love flow through me. May all that I am be one with you in love and in peace. Amen."

Say this as a prayer. Then recite the names of the Reiki symbols and perform your healings.

And each morning before you meditate, say these words:

"Dear Jesus, my friend and my protector, be with me now and through my day. Let your deep love embrace me, let forgiveness and compassion fill me. Let grace be mine. Amen."

Then do your mantra meditation. And throughout the day, say a little prayer to call me near: "Dear Jesus, come to me. Amen"

Do this and my presence will grow in your life, hourly, daily. Call me to you, not in desperation, but in love and communion. Just to be connected. Just to be.

I have been sleeping in the room nearby, but am now awakened and ready for active participation in your life.

Welcome. Shalom.

Until I started writing this chapter, I did not realize that my Jesus experiences had been so strongly related to Reiki. And that relationship continued, for my next encounter was when I went to Maui for my Karuna Reiki attunement in October, 2007, an experience I have shared in detail in the next chapter.

Meditative Sessions

What I find now is that Jesus will sometimes appear in sessions I am having with clients. In these cases, it is more reflective of the relationship he has to my client, than to me. Sometimes, for example, he has taken a client's hands to let her know that she has the power of healing flowing through her. Sometimes he has been there with his entire family, welcoming my client like the long-lost relative she truly is. And sometimes he is simply there, often along with

Mother Mary and Mary Magdalene, sending out his loving energy and his blessings.

What All This Means

I cannot say what this means or where it goes, only that it is clearly a blessing—and something I now accept as a part of my spiritual life.

At first I was hesitant to talk to anyone about these experiences—it seemed presumptuous of me to claim this personal relationship. But I have subsequently learned that this is considered standard practice for many Christians, to establish just this kind of individual, deeply personal, relationship with Jesus.

I have read some books about what biblical scholars think Jesus might really have said or done. Deepak Chopra wrote a wonderful book called *The Third Jesus*, which is an attempt to bring his teachings into a more timely understanding. But in the end, I just decided to do it my way, to have my own experience and not worry about what it might mean to anyone else.

Here is what I take away from it all:

- There is love, unconditional and indescribably deep, and it is there for us; we are truly loved beyond measure, whether we know it or not.
- There is a specific energy associated with Jesus, and it is all about that love, love that goes beyond forgiveness or tolerance and into complete acceptance of us exactly as we are.
- Regardless of what some scholars say, I can easily imagine that Jesus the man actually performed miracles. The flow of love that I felt

could heal anything; it could cause water to decide to become wine, just because it could.

- All that said, the Jesus I know does not ask to be worshipped; there is no need for any spiritual or religious belief in order to partake of the grace that flows.

This is yours to claim and own, this love. It is a love of power and grace. And it is there for you, right now, no matter what. There is nothing you can do to lose this love, try as you may. It is all yours, exactly as you are, with all that you have done and left undone. It is yours.

THE MAUI PAPERS

Ihave a very dear friend, Mary Keller, who has been with me every step of my spiritual journey. You may have met Mary in my book about my spiritual awakening, *There is a Garden*. She and I also went to Stonehenge together to become Usui Reiki Masters, my first encounter with Jesus.

And now Mary and I were again on a spiritual journey together, to become Karuna Reiki Masters in Maui. And again, Jesus would be central in the experience.

We stayed at the Hotel Hana Maui, a peaceful enclave with cottages overlooking the ocean. No television or radio, no computers. Just peace, beauty and the constant sound of the ocean striking the lava rocks below. Our cottage had a wide terrace with an incredible view, just grass, other peaceful cottages, swaying palm trees and the ocean.

For the first three days, Mary and I went to our class, a wonderful experience that included guided meditations, group healing sessions and attunements into Karuna Reiki.   For the last four days, we spent a lot of time on that terrace, just soaking in the Hawaiian rain, sun and ocean roar, as we did our own meditations and Reiki sessions.

My Journal

Below are entries from my Maui journal.

Thursday, October 4, 2007

We have arrived. I am now sitting on the veranda of my ocean view cottage at the Hotel Hana Maui with my dear friend Mary, who gave me this journal as a gift. Heaven!

∞

Friday, October 5, 2007, during Karuna Reiki class

I just had my first level Karuna Reiki attunement. Nothing dramatic. Just a peaceful feeling. I asked for the presence of Jesus and received it, but not in a dramatic way, just in a surrounding warmth with the words, "I am awake in your life," the same words I heard back in July.

"And thus are we transformed" is what just went through my mind. And now I see a long road stretching out in front of me. I am walking it alone, but with the sure knowledge that I am not alone at all.

∞

Saturday, October 6th, during Karuna Reiki class

We just had a lovely guided meditation. I walked through a thick forest, then across a green meadow under blue skies and up a hill. On the hill was an enormous crystal, as large as a house, sparkling and glowing in the sun. There was a door; I entered. Inside, the crystal house was bright and sparkling, full of angels and benevolent spirits, a place of true wonder. After a time I saw a treasure chest and knew that it contained something meant just for me.

I approached the chest and opened it. Slowly, two beings emerged, silvery white and glowing. After a moment I recognized that the one in the front, the smaller of the two, was Mary, Mother Mary, and she was somewhat merged with Jesus who was behind her and taller.

Mary came forward and embraced me with motherly love, an embrace so complete that it filled every place within me that needed filling. And I knew that she was not only here to fill me with love, but to act as a pathway to her son, an opening, a way to more easily access that energy that I seem to be so drawn toward.

And then I found myself lifted into the light. There I was, a little baby, held by loving and adoring parents. They were my parents, but transformed by love and free of their own fears. They held me and looked at me with such adoration. Oh, she is so perfect!

And I began to grow into an adult, deeply adored and appreciated for being exactly as I am, just me. As I grew I was surrounded by light and goodness, deeply in touch with many beings of light.

Then I knelt before Jesus and he baptized me, making the sign of the cross on my forehead. I could feel the cross etched deeply in my skin; no, deeper. And then I was enveloped in Mary's love and Jesus' love. All of my fears were completely healed and I felt myself in the arms of a deeply supporting, loving, motherly protection and yes, adoration.

And now, after the meditation, I can still feel the cross on my forehead.

∞

Sunday, October 7th, last day of Reiki class
We just had another guided meditation. This time, after emerging from the forest, we took a path to the left, up a high mountain to a sacred temple. I walked up the temple steps, and on each of the seven steps, felt my chakras clear, from root to crown.

The vast temple was full of enlightened beings including, of course, Mary and Jesus. Again, I knelt before Jesus and was baptized with the sign of the cross on my forehead. Again, I felt the sign go deeply within me.

I saw many statues inside the temple, several statues of Mary with her arms outstretched to accept and comfort. There were also crucifixions and a pieta, which made me feel uncomfortable at first, but whenever Jesus was seen on the cross or in Mary's arms, there was also movement, so it never seemed like suffering. It was instead a symbolic spiritual quickening.

Then the temple was full of enlightened beings and many, many angels. There was a clearing and cleansing. I forgave and I was forgiven. "I love you, I forgive you, I set you free."

I started to leave the temple, but then turned and ran back, ran through the temple and embraced and said goodbye to everyone. I was so full of pure love, it seemed impossible that I could actually leave.

And now, with the meditation over, I can still feel the cross on my forehead.

∞

This seems like the right time to ask my other question. What do the readers of my websites want and need from me?

And the answer comes: "The holy, the sacred. To be a portal to the mystical and to God."

∞

We meditate on Om.

I start to see a church, but it quickly dissolves. Now I am riding on a huge white bird, gliding over the ocean, dipping and soaring in zestful freedom as the wind blows through my hair.

And then I know the answer: true holiness requires freedom. This is what my readers want and need: holiness and freedom.

The Visions and Messages

In the following four days, I received several visions from Mary and Jesus as well as Quado messages on the topic of holiness and freedom. When I received the visions, words came at the same time, words I wrote down as they came to me.

∞

Monday, October 8th, 6 AM on the cottage terrace. A vision comes to me and I write it all down in my journal as it occurs.

Jesus appears, then Mary appears in front of him, holding out her hand. Come walk with us in the garden.

This is the tree of life. Its roots go deep into both earthly life and in faith, for it requires faith to sustain you through the trials and tribulations of this life.

But know that the love of God that flows is real, very real, as real as the stream that runs through the garden to water the tree. And if the love seems sometimes a flood that challenges all that you have and are, tearing at the roots and apparently eroding the very soil in which you grow, still it is love, love in the many guises and love in its many seasons. Still it is love.

And the fruit on the tree, this golden pear full of juice and joy, is the great and sacred love of life, for the more that you allow yourself to love life, the more you give yourself over to it, in storm or in flood, or when the river appears to disappear underground, the more the juice will flow in and gladden your heart.

You are here to live this life, as it is, as you are. You are here to embrace each moment, the lustful passions and the children that result, the meal set upon the table and the table filled only with faith, the stroll in the garden of plenty and the trek across the barren desert.

All of it is life. All of it is to be embraced and treasured. And when the golden pear appears not on the tree, so does it glow in your heart to sustain you. Let it be a part of your faith, a part of what pulls you and pushes you and drives you through.

You do not need answers. You need faith. And faith answers only with faith. And as you stand before this tree of life, see that you are one with it, your crown of leaves reaching to heaven, your feet firmly planted in faith and the golden pear glowing in your heart.

∞

Tuesday, October 9, 2007, 2 AM, on the cottage terrace. I awoke in the middle of the night with a feeling there was a message for me. I pulled out my laptop, so I could quickly capture every word as it flowed.

Carrie: I am getting the words holiness and freedom, that this is what the readers of our website and newsletters need. I would like to better understand exactly what is meant by this.

Quado answers: We have done much already to tell people about how to live a better life, calmer, more centered, a life lived within the moment. We have provided meditations to help lift people into a deep love of life and, most importantly, a love of themselves. We have centered our teachings around love and forgiveness, including a forgiveness of the self. We have also provided tools, through the power animal site, to help people make decisions based on intuition.

All of this is good and all of this stays. But yet, there is more.

The time has come to lift up into holiness. But it is to be a holiness based on freedom, not on restriction. There are no rules that surround this holiness. It is based solely on the deepest possible rivers of love and respect, a respect that reaches not only into respect for the self and others, but a respect for the holiness of every being that is, whether alive and walking this earth or in sprit form only. Holiness is recognition of the deep godliness of all. A deep recognition that everyone is an aspect of God, that there is no difference, there is no right or wrong, no better or worse, there simply is.

And there is a holiness that you can reach, that all can reach, which lifts them up beyond a place where they are sorting out the negative and positive, the light and the dark, and simply recognizing both sides as a part of the whole, one illuminating the other.

You begin in the darkness of ignorance. Then you proceed through a stage where you are training yourself to think positively, to come out of the past and future and into now, and all of this is good. All of this allows you to live a more peaceful and fulfilling life.

There comes a time when you are ready for the mystery. When you need to embrace the mystery and be lifted into it. There comes a time when you are ready to embrace faith completely, which means an utter cessation of asking why, for faith is the only answer. And a time when you cease to probe and explore the mystery, and simply allow yourself to be embraced by it. A time when you stop trying to drive the negative from your life, but begin instead to allow yourself now to be, to just be, with all sides of yourself as you are, all sides here within you, and recognize yourself for the goodness that you are.

And as you begin to do this, as you begin to accept all parts and aspects of yourself and see God shining within each one, as you begin to see God in the face of every person you encounter, even those you might have judged and found wanting, then you can begin the journey into holiness.

And the aspect of freedom that is so important here is that true holiness is not found by following rules. It is found by reaching down into your own heart and finding God there, letting that godliness fill you completely until you can feel the oneness that you are, and finding the guidance there.

We are seeking here to embrace the mystery, to walk in faith, to be the mystery and the godliness.

Experience God. Experience God within every atom of your being. Let every drop of dew on the rose shine with God, encompass God, and sing out God's praises. Let every line and pore on your body encompass and embrace God and godliness. Let every strand of hair on your head sway with godliness. Let the soil under your feet and the clouds floating across the sky sing out with godliness.

And if you are walking through the forest of wonder or in a deep fog of confusion and mystery, it does not matter. You can still learn to walk with God illuminating each step along the way.

There is a light that shines and it is you, and it is God and there is no difference. There is a heart that loves and it is you and it is God and there is no difference.

There is an angel at your shoulder and as you turn to look, it is you.

There is a cloud in the sky that writes your name large. You are in everything and everything is in you.

The dark, the light, the fullness and the emptiness, the mystery that cannot be solved is you. The faith that allows you to step out into the obscured mysteries of life with joy, that is you. That faith and courage reside in your heart.

And here, right here in this forest, with the furthest reaches shrouded in fog and mystery, only able to see a few trees and the barest suggestion of a path through the dense growth, here, in the heart of this deepening mystery, you begin to see that mystery begets mystery and that the journey in will uncover wonder, but no answers. Merely wonder. Merely godliness. Merely grace.

And it is this grace that is also a very large part of the holiness that we seek, for grace is given as a gift but never formed in any other way. Grace and faith walk hand in hand, for when the faith is great enough, the grace is granted and the next step is made clear.

The clarity of the forest lies deep within you and only the barest glimpses are given. The holiness lies in deep acceptance of this, so that after a time you come to love the fog of mystery, you come to realize that God is the mystery as well as the grace and the freedom and beauty that live within you.

And faith becomes a breath you take with each step as you embrace what is. And as you look behind you, you see flowers have sprung up in your footsteps, for you have left a path of grace and love through the mystery, a path others might follow if the freedom in their hearts lead them down the same path.

Holiness is completely separate from the circumstances of your life. Attainment of a deeply holy state does not mean that you are rich or poor, does not mean that you succeed or fail or fulfill goals you have set out for your physical attainment in this life. It does not mean you are good or bad, have broken rules or followed them, behaved yourself well according to society or behaved badly. None of this is relevant to your state of holiness.

For the freedom of true holiness allows you to set your own guidelines for what is truly right or wrong for you, on your path as you walk. And you walk in such a deep state of grace that you know that forgiveness is so complete that it is no longer even necessary, for there is nothing to forgive. How can forgiveness be required when there is no wrong to be righted, no mistake to be corrected? Forgiveness is granted in every moment, even as the words leave your mouth or the thought crosses your mind, even as you take action you later come to understand differently.

In a state of holiness, forgiveness and compassion are a ground state ingrained in your being, as natural and easy to you as each breath of faith that you take.

And God continues to sparkle in the eyes of each person you meet and grace is in each word they utter, for the holiness of each person shines out to you like a light.

I am this. You are this. We are this. And this is God. And grace flows.

∞

Tuesday, October 9, 2007 around 6:30 AM. As I sit on the veranda and watch the sun rise over Maui, a vision comes to me. I write it down in my journal as it occurs.

I see a landscape stretched out before me, but I must draw closer to see what it is. I sense it is another kingdom, but I am in a mist, unable to quite discern it.

Now an angel appears on each side of me. They lift me and we begin to fly toward this kingdom of light. Yes, I can see now that it is sparkling in light. We fly and fly toward it, yet still it is indistinct to me, just shapes and colors and features I can almost make out, but not quite.

Is there a waterfall? Perhaps. A desert? Perhaps.

And now we are within it, but it is like being within a cloud. The angels depart and leave me standing alone in the midst of this cloud.

Now Jesus appears before me and then in front of him, Mary. She reaches out a hand to me and says, "Come with us now into the kingdom of the heart."

The clouds glow with pink light as we walk into them. And now before me is a waterfall on the left, with lush green ferns growing on the surrounding rocks. The power of the falls subsumes all around it. It is all I can hear or see. I can feel the spray of the water on my face.

Jesus says, "My father is here," and a rainbow moves through the falls.

Then Mary gestures to the right, where a barren desert stretches out, mile after mile of sand, baked hard in the relentless sun. There is no water to be seen, just miles and miles of burning sand. I can feel the heat on my face.

Jesus says, "My father is here," and a lizard runs across the sand.

The clouds again form around me, glowing pink and gold. Then they clear. And as they clear, I see a fertile valley formed where the waterfall on the left poured into the desert on the right. The valley is teeming with life. The waterfall has provided enough water so that there are streams everywhere. Trees have sprung up fed by the water and golden pears of wisdom hang from the trees.

And over on the left, on a rock at the top of the waterfall, the lizard sits, sunning himself and smiling.

∞

Tuesday, October 9, 2007 around 11 PM. I am sitting in quiet contemplation when a vision comes to me. I write it down in my journal as it occurs.

Jesus appears before me, and then Mary before him. She reaches out her hand to me and says, "Come with us up the mountain."

There is snow on the rocks as we begin to climb. The wind is cold and blowing strongly, but still we climb. The rock is hard and the climb is steep, but it is somehow not overly difficult.

We stop before a cliff. There is a tree growing out of the cliff, just barely hanging on, its roots clinging to the rocks.

"So are the blessed," Jesus says.

We continue the climb. We stop before a craggy peak, where a majestic eagle sits. Suddenly he soars off into the clouds, his wings outstretched in beauty and power.

"So are the blessed," Jesus says.

And we continue to climb. The snow is heavier and we encounter a little bunny rabbit shivering in the snow. He hops away, frightened by our presence.

"So are the blessed," Jesus says.

And at the very top, the clouds clear and we see a verdant valley below. Many people live there, tilling the soil, picking fruit off the trees.

"So are the blessed," Jesus says.

Then we walk around to the other side of the mountain and below see a great city. Airplanes fly in and out. Ocean liners arrive and leave the port. Skyscrapers reach to the sky and cars clog the busy freeways.

The city is humming with enterprise and also struggling with poverty. We see the rich and the poor doing what the rich and the poor do. We see the privileged and the confident, the timid and the dispossessed, all doing what they do in a great city.

"So are the blessed," Jesus says.

And then he climbs to the very top, the highest rock on the highest peak, so that all is encompassed in his look and his outstretched arms, as he slowly rotates, his love and blessings flowing out and down upon the verdant valley and the humming city both.

And a momentary hush falls as the pink light flows down like a cloud. And for this moment, all of the people stop, touch their hearts and feel the blessing and the love, the love that cannot be surpassed and that never ends.

And then they pick up their plows and their briefcases, push their shopping carts and start up their cars, as if nothing had happened, nothing at all.

But a tiny pink remains in the air, just the lightest tinge of blessing. And here and there a few people pause again, look at the pink in the clouds, put their hands on their hearts and say a little prayer of thanks.

And this prayer causes the pink to expand and glow, enough so that a few more notice it. Some of these pause and some do not. But enough notice and enough give thanks that the love stays in the air and does not dissipate, stays in the air and in the breath, hangs over the busy activities and floats in the consciousness, never to be quite the same as before.

And as a little pink puff of love is about to dissolve, someone suddenly notices it and give thanks and causes it to glow and expand.

"So are the blessed," Jesus says.

∞

Wednesday, October 10, 2007, 5 AM.
Carrie: How are we to move into this state of holiness?

Quado answers: You will be guided, of course. And the guidance has already begun. The keys are meditation and contemplation.

Contemplation is important because this is holiness with freedom. You will not be given external rules to follow. You must learn to go within and find your own guidelines for behavior. This is a very personal holiness to be achieved and it requires your conscious and active involvement in the process.

Spend time contemplating sacred writings. You will find that they often ask questions about mystery, about faith, about God, rather than giving answers. That is because their purpose is to lead you to opening your mind so that you may then find your own answers.

You, Carrie, have begun to receive visions that can serve as contemplations for others. This will continue. We will not interpret these visions or try to explain them. Instead we will offer them up as sacred contemplations, to be taken by each person and interpreted in their own way, turned into a holy meaning that is personal, that is deep, that is worthy of this precious life.

And then, throughout the day, you may each begin to live your life a bit differently by watching always for the God that is speaking through each person you encounter and the God that is present in each place you go.

If you look, you will see. If you seek this presence within each moment, you will find it.

Holiness is utter simplicity. It is a way to live that cares not for the circumstances and situations of your life. It does not matter if you are caught in traffic, shopping for groceries, paying the bills or contemplating a perfect sunset. This is your life and it is holy. This moment contains God, for you are one with the wonder and glory that is God. You are God.

And as such, how could this moment not be holy? And the others who surround you, in the car that just cut in front of you, or pushing the grocery cart ahead of you in line, or on the telephone asking you for payment of a charge that you did not incur, these people are holy as well, each and every one. The soldiers in battle, on both sides, are holy, as holy as the monks privileged to be in the distant monastery. All are holy. You cannot help it. They cannot help it. It is what you are.

Our goal here is not to change who and what you are, for that cannot be changed. Our goal is to guide you to finding the holiness inside yourself and others and then to allowing it to express itself through the actions you take in your life. Every moment is a choice you make about how you will spend the precious second that has been granted you in this lifetime.

But do not interpret this as a suggestion that you must change the work that you do, that there are some professions nobler than others. All work done with integrity is noble. The answer is to reach a state of integrity with what you do and to infuse your every thought and action with holiness, which is simply the recognition of the presence of God in everything.

It is simplicity itself.

∞

After the above message from Quado, I went out on the veranda, to watch the sun rise over the ocean. I traced the Karuna Reiki clairvoyance-enhancing symbol over my third eye, an action that had triggered the previous visions. I then received two visions, both of which I recorded in my journal as they came to me.

Mary appears, standing in front of Jesus. She holds out her hand and says, "Come with us now, down into the cave, this tomb of kings."

We enter a cave, dark but spacious. As my eyes adjust, I see that there is some light inside, though I cannot see its source. The air is cool and still. We walk soundlessly across the cool stone floor in the dim light.

Jesus points to the tomb of a king. He was greatly revered and his tomb is covered with stories of his greatness.

"So are the blessed," Jesus says.

We continue walking. He points to another tomb, this one in disrepair. The writings indicate that this was a cruel king, hated and feared, a man responsible for much suffering.

"And yet he is blessed," Jesus says.

Then I see a spirit rising from this tomb, aglow with light, glorious to behold. Angels surround the spirit and sing. I look back to the other tomb and see the same thing, a beautiful glowing spirit surrounded by angels.

The spirits move forward to the center of the cave and merge, becoming one in light and love. Then they are lifted to the light, up through the roof of the cave into the heavens. They are one spirit, one light.

And I am alone in the cave, standing on the cool stones as a fresh breeze blows gently through.

∞

That vision dissolves and now the second vision comes.

Mary appears with Jesus standing behind her. She holds out her hand and says, "Come with us now to the battlefield."

We are suddenly in the midst of a fierce battle. Soldiers are shooting, running for cover, shooting more. From this vantage point, dropped into this as we were, it is impossible to tell what they are fighting for. But they are dressed differently and it is clear to them who is on which side.

Now I see through the eyes of one soldier. His vision is cloudy. He is in a state of shock, responding only from his training. Then I see through the eyes of a soldier on the other side and it is the same. With the loud sounds, the movement fast and confusing, the dust flying in the air, the experience is even beyond fear. It is beyond what is human and real.

And then for one moment the two soldiers I am within come around the corner and see each other, face to face. Hatred and fear flash across their eyes as they reach for their guns. But it is like slow motion, for Jesus has motioned to a ring of angels who descend, surrounding them. As they raise their weapons, their vision suddenly clears and they see each other as people, as men who can still fall in love and father children, till the soil and watch the sun rise.

This recognition brings tears to their eyes and they turn from each other, back as they came.

Then the angels disappear and the battle continues, the outcome uncertain.

∞

After I returned home from the Maui retreat, I had one more Jesus vision, and then a follow-up session with Quado to talk about the meaning of it all. Again, the following is from my journal.

∞

October 27, 2007. I make the Karuna Reiki clairvoyance symbol over my third eye, and receive the following:

Jesus appears and then Mary before him. She reaches out her hand to me. "Come with us now to the great storehouses of wisdom, where the truth is writ large for all to see."

Then Jesus leads the way, walking into room after room made of stone. Each room is full of books, covered in dust. Then we progress further back in time and the rooms are full of parchment scrolls.

Everything is dusty and apparently untouched for years. There are no footprints in the dust on the floor. There has been no one in these rooms for many,

many years, for hundreds, perhaps thousands, of years.

Jesus stops and pulls out a parchment scroll. "This I said," he says, and the scroll turns to dust in his hand.

He reaches for another. "This I did not say," he says. And this scroll also turns to dust in his hand.

"But it matters not. For my words are not important. The truth is writ large in the heart. And this requires no scholars to find."

He looks around the room, then sweeps his hand through the air, turning all to dust. "Too much has been made of my words already. Would that I could take them all away."

Then he sweeps his hand through the air and all the bibles and scholarly treatises in the entire world turn to dust.

"So let it be. So let it be only that love shines and peace lives in each heart. The rest does not matter." And with that he turns and is gone.

Mary looks at me, almost apologetically, as if to excuse her son's manners. "He grows tired of it," she says.

But then she smiles, a smile full of love and peace, revealing a great inner serenity. "Love," she says. And then she too disappears.

∞

November 16, 2007. Carrie to Quado: What does this energetic presence of Mary and Jesus mean to us?

Quado Answers: Mary's role is that of the opening portal, a way to ease into energy that may yet be too strong for you to access directly. Jesus has a vital energetic presence, but it is not relaxed and friendly. It is more authoritarian, an authority stemming from a deep truth that is deeply and urgently understood to its core. It is seeking expression, yes, but not dilution and compromise. There is no compromise felt here in this energy.

You are being called to lift yourself up to this level, the level that will truly reveal what is being offered. And you can do this simply by opening yourself to it, by not fighting it, by not questioning whether it is real. It is real. It is vitally real.

Is it demanding? Yes, it is far more demanding than my energy, for I will reach down and pick you up, no matter where you lie. This is energy that asks you to reach deeply into yourself and find your strength. It is energy that demands responsibility from you. It is energy that asks you to find your own power and step up, walk up the temple steps and bid the doors to open. This is what this energy asks of you.

You know that it is loving energy. You have felt this. But you also know that the love here is deeply intense. It is not just a warm blanket of comfort, as I am. It is a hot love, a love that burns away the unnecessary and the trivial. It is an intense glow that demands your full attention in its presence. It is not casual. It is not relaxing or relaxed.

And it is not an energy that is concerned with the fulfillment of your wishes, with your wealth or status or anything that is merely confined to the details of your life. It is concerned only with your soul, with the reaching and yearning of your deepest inner truth. It is an energy that wants you to ache and yearn for oneness with God, and then to express this oneness in all that you do and say and think, in everything that you are.

For it is an energy that recognizes the ultimate truth, that you are God, you are a full expression of God in every moment, and that your power is therefore limitless, if you will only knock on the temple door and ask to be admitted.

But do not expect that you will be the same, that you will or can emerge from the temple the same person who entered. The voices inside have much to say, but their utterances are life-altering.

The invitation has been issued. You may stand here on the steps with the wind whipping around you, hearing that call, or you may complete your climb and knock. It is up to you, all of you, whether you care to answer the ultimate call to holiness and freedom.

And this freedom is a freedom from all the rules and restrictions you thought would give you entrance. They are not relevant. The truth resides only within you. And the steps that one may walk are not the same steps for all. They are individual and true, deep in your heart and soul.

There is a call deep within you, an ultimate yearning that is so much greater than the yearning you have had for material comfort and safety. There is an ultimate yearning for this entrance into the holy of holies, this joining and oneness that will feel like completion. But you must walk these steps alone, fueled by your own strength, guided by your own vision.

Come. The greatest part of your journey still lies ahead.

AN EXTRAORDINARY
YEAR BEGINS

I would like to tell you now the story of an extraordinary year in my life, a year in which I was led, step by step, from person to person, into amazing experiences, each building upon the one before in unexpected ways. It is a period of my life that exemplifies that state of grace in which we can live, if only we allow ourselves to be led without demanding that we understand why or where.

It all began in early July, 2008. I was working on a consulting gig that was expected to go through September. The drive was about an hour on the freeway, which for Los Angeles is not bad at all. The people were nice and the work was fairly undemanding, just improving the company's use of a computer system. And yet, for some reason, there were days when I found myself with tears streaming down my face as I drove.

I have since come to recognize this feeling. It is not like the depression you may feel when things have not gone your way. Instead, it is a kind of soul sadness, as if you are observing your own life and it makes you deeply sad that you are not doing what you are truly meant to do.

I had just started to get an inkling that there were, in fact, some extraordinary things that I was meant to do—or so it seemed from a vision quest I had gone on shortly before.

My Vision Quest

Back in May, 2008, I had been traveling across the US doing computer training sessions and one day, somewhere in Maryland, I felt strongly that I should go to a local bookstore. I had been feeling restless about books, looking at rack after rack of books in the airport bookstores and feeling that there was one I was seeking. And here I was in Maryland, suddenly knowing that the book I wanted was nearby.

The hotel desk directed me to the nearest bookstore. I walked in and immediately went to a table of non-fiction hardbacks near the entrance. Then I just ran my hand across the books, and when I got to *Steering by Starlight*, by Martha Beck, my hand said, "This is it." So I bought it and began working my way through it as I traveled across the country.

I launched a 30-day visioning period, as the book suggested. It became my morning routine to walk through the steps and write down the resulting visions in my journal. Here's a brief summary of Martha's steps:

- Sit quietly with your journal nearby; breathe deeply and relax
- Close your eyes and focus on the space between your eyes. Allow that space to expand, wider and wider
- Feel that openness and expansion in your entire body as you expand out and become one with all that is
- Now, ask for three visions by projecting yourself out into your future, a place where everything is exactly as it is meant to be. Picture how things are in this wondrous future with regards to Love, Fulfilling Adventure and Meaningful Work.
- Write down what you see.

In my case, several patterns began to emerge. For Love, I saw myself having fun, dancing, singing and talking with a group of women. The Adventure visions were of me doing highly physical things that, frankly, don't much appeal to me: going down the rapids, taking a hot air balloon ride, crossing a ravine on a rope bridge, that sort of thing. (I have conveniently set aside the Adventure visions as less important.)

In the Meaningful Work visions, I saw myself traveling and then standing in front of large audiences, on the stage in front of thousands of people. It felt exactly right, as if this was, in fact, what I was meant to do. The details were different from vision to vision, but this was the common theme.

This vision of the stage was actually quite familiar. Some years before, I had attended a Deepak Chopra week-long meditation conference. He had walked us through an exercise where we were to picture ourselves fulfilling our deepest purpose. And there I was, just as I saw myself now, standing on a stage under bright lights, facing an audience of thousands. Then as now, I did not see exactly what I was doing on that stage. It was my hope in both cases that I was singing, but that was not clear.

A Voice Speaks

The vision of a large audience was also consistent with an experience I had in June of 2006. I was sitting outside in the late evening, relaxing, when I suddenly heard a voice inside my head. It wasn't my friend Quado. This voice was more authoritative: someone who speaks when he chooses to, not when you ask; someone who says what he has to say and then moves on, not someone who sticks around for questions.

I asked who it was and the answer came: "I am he who is without a name."

So I said, "Hold it right there!" and ran to get my journal. Then I came back and asked him if he would be kind enough to start over.

Below is what he said. Incidentally, the 'Maureen' he refers to is Maureen Moss, who has since developed the World Puja radio network, on www.worldpuja.org.

Carrie. You will fulfill your highest intention in the next thirty earth years. The highest intention, that you have been working toward for centuries, will be fulfilled.

It will be revealed to you as you go along, of course, but know this: your highest intention and that of Maureen involves the lifting of many spirits, from one level to multiple levels higher.

Your intentions are so strong and your power so great, that your concerns over money and success are laughable. They seem so serious and so real to you, but they are illusion, complete illusion.

Your intention and purpose are so strong that you are deeply empowered toward their fulfillment. And all you need to do is respond to the next thing that flows toward you with deep integrity and great courage. You need do nothing more. For you are now fully riding the flow of your intended life, which means that it will all come to you. Yes, you will need to work hard, but it will also be pleasure.

Carrie. It is very important that you understand your purpose here. Maureen understands hers more clearly, but you are clinging to some old perceptions.

Yes, you have one foot in each world, and that is very important for you to be able to communicate with a wider audience. But as you keep one foot in this physical, earthly world, do not be seduced by it. You are a higher being, in the last stages of your evolution, as is Maureen. And your strong ties to the physical achieve this purpose of communication, but do not indicate a lower level of evolution and energetic presence. It will also allow you to remain in this world for a longer duration, which is right for what you are to do.

So let us be clear. You, both of you, are here to shine out with a brighter light and a higher frequency, enough so that you will lift millions of people to a higher level. Yes, the two of you will accomplish this. This is your higher intention and you have all the power you require to fulfill it.

What are you learning about yourself, Carrie? You can take the complex and make it understandable. But it is even more. Lift and shine. Lift and shine.

And that was that; I have never heard this voice again.

So what do you do, when you see visions of yourself in front of an audience of thousands, when voices speak to you of lifting millions of people, and yet your daily life consists of driving on the freeway to a boring job, when your soul is crying out to be moving toward a larger purpose, but yet you see no path toward it?

You just live. You get ready and then watch and wait. And you remember, always, that spirit does not work on our timetable. From the point of view of spirit, everything is happening at once; there is no waiting, no ticking clock, no linear time stretching out ahead. After all, from a soul perspective, if it doesn't happen in this lifetime, there is always the next one, and the one after that.

And you sing as you drive on the freeway; you slow down each time you walk under a tree and take a deep breath; you quite literally take time to smell the roses. In short, you do your very best to find joy in each moment as it comes.

Change Happens

I should mention here that at this time, I was consulting for the same company where I began this story. The Screamer was no longer there. In fact, there were only a few people left from those days and when we ran into each other, we would laugh and trade stories of about how amazingly awful she had been. The painful past had become a series of highly entertaining anecdotes.

But The Screamer had also left a legacy, a corporate culture that was, you might say, a little edgy. And so it was not a complete surprise when my consulting engagement was suddenly terminated--*with three days notice!* — as they decided one day they needed to cut expenses.

As I walked out of the building to my car, carrying my little box of possessions, I felt as if an enormous weight had been lifted from my shoulders. I wanted to run to the car and cry out my freedom with joy. In spite of my quite legitimate concern over having no income, it felt exactly right to be leaving this job and launching into — well, perhaps into my vision, stepping on that stage. After all, anything could happen!

Wouldn't it be a wonderful story to tell you that I walked away from that same company, having been let go for the second time, and this time, walked in joy directly into the future I had seen in my visions? Wouldn't that be fabulous?

But it didn't happen quite that way.

Throughout July, I often awakened in great anxiety, with fear just coursing through my body. Then I would spend a couple of hours in contemplation and meditation, bringing myself back to center and peace. I looked unsuccessfully for consulting work. We lived off my receivables, and when they were gone, off the 401K. We got by.

Looking back in my journal, I see that August was marked by a lot of shifts in direction, trying this and that, a lot of swings between fear and enthusiasm, and generally driving my poor husband crazy.

On August 11th, there is an interesting journal entry, as I was asking Quado (again!) what I should do with my life long-term. The answer was this:

Speaking. A Call to Greatness. A book, seminar, workshop.

This was my first hint moving me toward the writing of this book. But it would be nearly a year before it truly began to flow, a year in which I had many things I needed to experience, before I would even know what it was I wanted to say to you in this book. And a year in which I needed to undergo significant expansion toward my own greatness.

In late August, 2008, I attended a conference for aspiring speakers, because of a strong feeling that I needed to attend. Finally, on the last day, Gary deRodriguez spoke about Humanistic NLP. Ah, at last, the reason I was here! I soaked up every word and then went to his website, downloaded some videos and began his 90-day Conditioning program (see my earlier chapter, "Your Morning Routine").

For the next forty days, I went through a great period of transformation. I painted the house in beautiful colors, learning new techniques like Venetian plastering and sponging. I dieted and exercised and took off ten pounds. I began singing again. I felt such a strong flow of energy growing within me, like a golden channel of light from my soul self above me, running straight down my body, connecting me to that higher soul energy at all times.

Yes!

And there I was, gloriously unemployed, buoyant and joyful, even as the economy was beginning to collapse around us, as it did so resoundingly in the Fall of 2008. Every headline that cried out doom and dismay looked to me like another door opening, another way that the old was making room for the new. As more people were plunged into fear, I returned to posting daily Quado messages on my website, to do what I could to keep people's spirits high.

Here is one of my favorite Quado Messages from that time, entitled "Yes!"

Look around. Look around with new eyes. For every wall that has fallen, a passageway now exists that did not exist before. A barrier has been removed and the open vista of life stretches out ahead.

Do not stare down at the stones that lie broken and crumbling beneath your feet. Look out. Lift your eyes and see that this fallen wall is now a portal that you can walk through.

See how the walls that you thought were bringing you stability and safety were actually blocking you from walking your path more fully, more vibrantly, out in the sunshine of life. See how the open vista beckons you, how your heart yearns to walk free, out in the sunshine, carrying only a packet full of faith.

See the others who are out on the path, how their steps are beginning to pick up vigor as they begin to see that they can not only survive, but in fact can thrive, out in the open fields of life, free of the heavy walls that others put up around them over the centuries.

Look around. Look around with new eyes and see your life opening up around you. Step out of the rubble and be glad that your prison has crumbled and the guards are looking away, their eyes clouded with self-pity over their losses.

Look around and sense the wind of freedom that is blowing across the land. See how it stirs up the dust and blows it away. See how the light pouring in now through the fallen wall exposes the dust and cobwebs in which you have been living, the moldy old ways of thinking and seeing and being.

Step outside these crumbling walls and feel the fresh wind of promise, of newness. "Yes, yes!" it calls. "Yes!" rings out across the land. "Yes!" each bird sings.

Step out here and take a deep breath, look around and then say "Yes!" Say "Yes!" to life as it unfolds before you in wonder. This is the springing open wide. This is the opening and unfolding. This is the wonder of the becoming.

This is the moment to feel the greatness within you, to dip down into your heart of courage and pull out all of your talents, your deep abilities, your glory and beauty and wonder. Pull it all out; lift it up to the opening vista of life and say: "Yes, yes! I am ready to live, to move into my greatness, to open to all that I am and let it shine out. Yes, I am here. I am ready. I am."

LEVELS OF EXISTENCE

This forty-day period of transformation brought me to a place where I felt I could be of service. The joy that I felt, in spite of everything happening to and around me, was something I wanted to share. And so, I offered Soul Sessions to my clients.

Before I tell you about the Soul Sessions, however, I would like to share a vision I received some years before, so that you may understand what I mean when I speak of the soul.

∞

On October 17, 2000, I took my journal down to my garden for my usual morning conversation with Quado. On this particular day, however, instead of words filling my mind, I had a vision in my inner sight.

I saw a shadowy land the color of dark grey smoke. This was the world we inhabit, this physical life, where we live out our days with these changing bodies, these active minds and quirky personalities, these hearts full of tears and laughter.

Some of us were shining brightly from within, like beacons within the near-darkness, lighting the space around us with a golden glow. Some of us were barely visible, like dark shapes moving in the shadows. Most of us were flickering with light, sometimes barely lit and sometimes gleaming brightly, a flash here and a flash there.

Above this land of shadow was another level of existence, radiant and luminous, like the sky full of glorious sunshine that suddenly appears when an airplane rises above the clouds. Within this level were very large, intensely bright, golden balls of energy. And I knew these brilliant balls of energy, light and love to be our soul selves, the part of us that is eternal, outside time and space, the part of us that will still shine out even after this physical life has ended.

I saw then that each person in the shadow world of physical existence had a cord that reached up to one of these radiant souls. The people who were shining brightly in the shadows had a cord that was broad, strong and full of light, so that they were continually refreshed by a steady flow of dazzling love from their soul self on the higher level.

I saw one woman sitting in the lotus position in deep meditation; her body had a bright glow that extended far beyond her body, providing light for everyone around her. The cord connecting her to her higher self was broad and luminous, full of sparkling golden energy.

I saw others whose cords were badly tangled and twisted and to whom very little light was flowing; these people were lost and floundering, in pain and confusion.

And most of us, as we flickered in and out of light, had cords through which some light and love were pouring down, but not steadily. And we had our moments of pain, when the cord became tangled, and our moments of great love and joy, when the flow was open and pouring into us.

I could see that our happiness and joy were directly related to the flow of light and love from our souls, not to our activities and circumstances in the shadow world. And I could see that this was the one thing that was always there, that was ours to own our entire life, this great source of love and light, ever glowing above us.

And no matter whether someone flickered or glowed, their soul self was just as bright as any other. I saw that every person on the earth has a soul self of love and light, glowing brightly above. Everyone, without exception, has a cord that reaches up into this endless and vast source of loving energy. Everyone, without exception, is an extension of love and light. And that includes you, no matter what your life is or has been. And that includes everyone else, no matter what you may think of how they live or have lived.

Up on the higher level, that of the soul self, everything is connected in love. Up at that level, the soul of everyone you have ever known is there next to you, whether or not they are still in your life on the physical level. People you have yet to meet in this lifetime are glowing alongside your soul. Children you had or might have had, past lovers, grandparents long gone, casual acquaintances and best friends, bosses and coworkers, people you loved deeply and people who challenged you greatly, all are there and still glowing beside you in light and love.

I could see how intuition works, why we are able to understand what another is feeling, for we are, in fact, connected to them on this level. The act of breathing down into meditative space is really a lifting up into this soul space we share.

And I could feel so strongly that nothing is lost, ever. On this level, you are glowing together in love, no matter what has happened below. There can be no regret and no blame, for nothing is ever lost. There is no need for forgiveness, for everything is completely resolved within love, the love that has always been and always will be, connecting us to each other.

And then, suddenly, I saw a level higher, where everything was one blindingly bright light, without any individual differentiation. And this light was what some call God or the godhead, and others call oneness, beingness or the great all. And it was endless, eternal and limitless, an intensely bright, golden glowing light, all light, all love, without boundaries and without end.

And I knew that we exist at all three levels in every moment: in the great oneness and connection we call God; as separate soul selves of light and energy a level below; and as people here in the physical level, with bodies, minds and personalities that exist in linear time and then dissolve back into the higher level when our span of linear time is completed.

And as I looked again at the souls and the shadow world below them, I began to see and understand more. I saw that one soul has created, is connected to, multiple lives. These lives are in different dimensions in the shadow world, appearing to us to be past lives or future lives, but they all exist at once to the timeless soul. And at the level of the soul, all of them can be accessed, for they all exist at once, in the blink of an eye of the eternal soul.

I also saw that some souls had created spiritual entities, bright glowing forms within the shadow world, there to help and guide us, to teach us how to open wide the flow of love and light that is there for us at all times, pouring down from our souls. Perhaps my friend Quado is one of these.

THE SOUL SESSIONS

In October, 2008, right around the time of the Quado "Yes!" message, I began conducting private sessions to lift people up into their soul selves, so that we might see there the full power of our greatness and understand better how to express that greatness in this lifetime. And what I saw, through my very own personal experience, was unlike any belief system I am aware of.

These sessions not only gave me a new insight into who we are and what we are doing here in this lifetime, but they were also the source of amazing connections, leading me step by step into further adventures and understandings.

Nearly all of the Soul Sessions I conducted were remote, done over the telephone. In these sessions, I would enter a deeply meditative state and speak aloud of what I saw, felt and experienced.

Each session began with an energy clearing, just like the one I described earlier, where we picture a cone of gold and silver particles of light, swirling around and lowering gradually over the body, through the intuition (space between the eyes), the mind, the throat center of self-expression, the heart, the solar plexus and then the entire body. I used this time to get deeply connected with the energies and to observe areas of particular strength in my client.

Since this is an intuitive adventure, I never know where it will lead. There were sessions where I didn't even make it through the energy clearing before we were swept off into an adventure. I remember one in particular, with Marita, where I saw the energy swirling down to her hands. Then Jesus appeared, took her hands in his, and took over the entire session. Not surprisingly, this session led us to the understanding that she has much stronger healing powers than she had realized.

In most cases, after the energy clearing, I would see the soul self as a bright golden ball shining above each person's head. The energy of that soul self would then expand and invite us in. We would lift up into the expanding soul where a wondrous landscape would then appear and reveal itself to us, the landscape of the soul.

Soul Landscapes

The only way I can describe what I mean by a soul landscape is to give you examples of a few. So please allow me to introduce Wanda, Ervene, Karen and Sabina, four souls with very different landscapes.

Wanda was one of the first instances where I began to understand the connection to previous lifetimes. When we lifted up into Wanda's soul, we found a vast jungle. As we walked through the jungle, we discovered that the other lives of her soul had been healers. As each of these lives had transitioned back to the soul, they had buried a box containing everything they had learned during a lifetime of healing: potions, herbs, symbols and incantations. During meditation, Wanda may walk through the pathways in the jungle. When she steps upon one of the spots where a box is buried, all of the knowledge will be energetically transferred to her, flowing up from her feet and through her entire body. She may then use this knowledge during her own healing sessions, following the direction of her intuition. And when Wanda's life on earth is complete, she will take everything she has learned, put it in a box and bury it in the jungle to be passed on to another life.

Ervene's soul space was not earthbound in any way. At first we could just see light-bodies moving around. Then we saw that her soul spirals up and up, higher and higher, until she dissolves into the oneness. And this is the delight and passion of her soul, to reach up into the oneness and be with it and within it, and then to spiral this energy down into Ervene. The spiral is a glowing white light, incandescent; it extends several feet out from her body, and as she builds it, it shines out for miles. Ervene transforms the world around her simply by being and glowing and keeping her channel to her soul open.

When we lifted up into Karen's soul landscape, I was a bit startled, for it seemed to be a barren desert. But the desert began to transform, and we saw Karen's special gift. She can look out on the barren desert, with its dry cracked surface, and to her, it's full of seeds, buried under the cracked earth. And then, when she looks at a seed, she can see it fully realized. She can see the redwood here and the lily there, as they will be when they are watered and grow into their full selves. And what is more, Karen is herself the waterfall; she has the ability to create, to birth, to give life, to that seed.

Sabina's soul space felt very gentle and sweet, very soft. It immediately expanded out, to show us a circle of souls. Then we saw that within each of the souls, in the center of each glowing golden ball of light, was a beating heart. These beating hearts pump out love, all beating in the same rhythm. Sabina's soul has a great longing to join up with the other hearts who beat in the same rhythm, for when they do so, they create powerful waves of love that flow across the earth and out into the universe, transforming the world through love.

Observations and Conclusions

You may read the transcripts of many more soul landscapes in the Appendix at the end of this book. I would like to share now some observations and conclusions that I drew after spending time in the soul landscapes of over 80 clients.

Clarity, Certainty, Greatness and Power

You may be confused about your life, but your soul is not. There was a great sense of clarity and certainty in every soul I visited. I also learned that everyone, without exception, has greatness within, a vast and endless supply of creativity and power.

If I were to visit your soul, I know that I would feel that same sense of certainty and power. It seems to be the ground state, the foundation from which we grow and expand into this life.

I would wish for you that you may open to your soul self and learn to know yourself in your glory. It is all there, waiting for you to experience and to pour down into this body, this life. In the final chapter of this book, I have written specific steps you may take to fully access the greatness that is within you. But remember always that you have no need to strive for greatness, for it was granted to you at your birth.

Success, Money and Achievement

I was not actually that surprised to learn that we are all full of greatness and power; I had suspected as much. But I was very surprised to learn that this power does not necessarily lead to money and recognition, to what we are so used to thinking of as success and achievement.

A very important observation from these sessions is that at the soul level, there appears to be no particular interest in this aspect of our lives at all. The talents your soul has given you may make some careers more appropriate than others, but there is very wide latitude in what you might do with your life. And in many cases, most cases, what you choose to do for a living and how good you are at it, appears to be simply a matter of free choice, irrelevant to your soul.

This idea takes a bit of getting used to, since it runs completely against what our present-day society teaches, at least in the West. We have been taught to worship at the altar of success, if not for wealth, at least for individual achievement, to be all you can be, to go for it, to stretch, to utilize all your gifts to the fullest, to fulfill your potential. And yet, from what I saw and learned, in soul after soul, there is no such higher directive.

Please pause a moment and reflect on this, for the implications are enormous. It may well be that your soul is absolutely delighted with how you are living right now, even though television and magazines, your family, friends and coworkers, may be urging you to accomplish more.

Your Soul's Delight
Rather than thinking of the soul as a stern parent who has laid out a task for you to accomplish, consider thinking of your soul as carefree and fun-loving, full of joy and light, love and adventure. Rather than having given you an assignment, a purpose you need to fulfill during your time here, this fun-loving and adventurous soul may simply have a delight, something that gives her pleasure. And you may be an extension of that, someone spun out into the ether to have an adventure on this earth during this lifetime, for the sole purpose of delighting your soul.

Now having said that, I must also say that I encountered some souls with a strong intention that they wished to see fulfilled. But that intention most often related to love and connection, and was achieved through meditation, not through ambition and hard work.

Be-ers and Do-ers

Along this same line, one of the most surprising discoveries for me was that some people are not meant to do anything tangible at all. I gradually came to understand that there are some people who achieve their purpose simply by being, not by doing.

I am a Do-er. I enjoy completing projects and tasks, like writing books and creating CDs. If you give me a deadline, I will become even more productive. That is naturally who I am, and I am fortunate that it is also highly rewarded in our society.

I have often been frustrated by people who are not like me, who move at a different pace, who do not seem to accomplish as much as I think they should. What I discovered during the Soul Sessions, however, was that these Be-ers are meant to be who they are, just as they are, doing what they do easily and well: simply being. In fact, I became quite fond of the Be-ers — and even a bit envious.

I encountered some souls whose energy was completely vertical. They were meant only to open themselves to the light, to reach and reach upward until they touched the hem of God. Although we all benefit from the light and love these people funnel down to us, they are not meant to "do" anything with it. The love that they spread in our world is simply a wonderful side-effect of their reaching energy, of the fulfillment of their mission.

If you are a Be-er, and not a Do-er, you know it already. It has probably been a source of some conflict in your life, since you are told constantly to set and meet goals, and yet deep inside you know that this kind of focused action does not work well for you. And to you I say, be who you are.

The people I met whose souls were Be-ers were so relieved to discover that it was all right to be as they were. If you are a Be-er, consider just staying in that non-competitive job so that you have energy at the end of the day to relax and enjoy the sunset. Stop striving to achieve that promotion. Move at your own pace. And if this means that you do not earn as much money, then just adjust your lifestyle accordingly, so that you are not overburdened with debt. Your greatness has already been granted to you; you have nothing to prove.

Multiple Lives and Soul Circles
In many Soul Sessions, after we had a look around the individual soul landscape, we expanded out to see the soul circle. What I saw most often was something like this: The soul is like a large glowing sun, surrounded by smaller stars. These shining stars are the lives the soul has spun out; they are tethered to the soul with arcing lights. I had a sense that the different lives might not share the same time and space on earth, but there was nothing definite about this. To the soul, there is no linear time, and so all of these lives exist at once. But to us here on earth, we might think of the other stars that attach to your soul as previous and future lifetimes.

These various stars, or lifetimes, all seem to share the same delight. If you are a be-er, a blossoming flower sending out the perfume of love, the other lives are likely to be the same. If you are a healer able to walk through a forest of healing knowledge, then the other lives have put that knowledge there during their earth adventure, and when you transition back to your soul-star state, you will place your knowledge in the forest as well.

Now, expand your vision out further and see that your soul-sun and its star-lives are part of a greater circle of souls, each surrounded by its own stars. These suns are connected not only with their own star-lives, but also with each other. In some cases, I saw highly intertwined systems of light, all arcing across and sharing energy. I had the sense that the souls that have joined in a soul circle share the same delight and intention for the lives they have created.

Some of the lifetimes spun out by the souls within your soul circle will share the same earth space and time with you. Where this is the case, it may well be that the intention your soul has given you for this lifetime is to connect with these other lives, those who are, in effect, your soul mates. In same cases, I saw that the connected lives had high-reaching goals, to create energy that would transform the world. In other cases, the purpose seemed to be simply to join with each other, not to achieve a particular purpose.

Some of the soul circles were vast. Some were very small. Some souls were meant to meet each other through meditation only, not necessarily to share an earth experience. Others were meant to know each other during their lives, possibly for long relationships, possibly for a short time only.

I would like to make an observation about soul mates and soul circles. When you meet someone and feel that deep, instant connection, when you just know that you have met a soul mate, someone within your soul circle, do not assume that this means you must have a close or long-lasting relationship during your life. Enjoy the recognition and connection for the time it is there, but let it be as it naturally is, and when its time is over, let it go.

Your Mission and Delight
I believe that you know who you are, the greater direction you are to follow and the delight of your soul. You may have been denying it, because others find it unacceptable or because it requires a lifetime change that appears overly challenging. But I believe you know.

If you have a particular calling, like some I met who were natural healers or teachers, you probably have at least an inkling. If you feel drawn to simply live, to reach up to God or to spread love like flowing water, then this is what you are meant to do. If you feel a burning drive to explode with knowledge like a volcano or fireworks lighting up the sky, then this is what you are meant to do.

The confusion lies not with your soul or your knowledge of who you are, but with the difference between that and what everyone else has told you all your life. You are full of power, talent and creativity. You are full of greatness. You may simply need to redefine that greatness so that it makes sense in light of who you truly are.

THE YEAR CONTINUES

Among the people who contacted me for a soul session were several that I felt connected to in some way; I felt that perhaps we were meant to do something together. Some of us have connected and taken a few steps together. With some, our time for joint adventure has not yet come. But here is what has occurred so far, as a direct result of the Soul Sessions.

Galactic Sisterhood

For a time, ten of us met weekly in a conference call. Allow me to introduce this group briefly (you may read further about them in the Appendix):

- Bernadette Wright, a do-er of immense power, who can transform a boulder into pure spirit and then manifest it into new forms at will
- Char Thomas, whose soul is full of gems she holds to the light, gems of truth, beauty and wisdom

123

- Christine Fotheringham, a quiet grove of trees, meant to live in stillness and contemplation
- Doreen Agostino, whose soul landscape holds towering gemstones, as big as castles and full of wisdom
- Ervene Boyd, who is a spiral of white light touching God
- Linda Hildebrandt, who is meant to explode like fireworks into the night sky, over and over
- Nancy Saar, a Be-er who is meant to bloom in love, letting the flowers of her heart send their perfume out into the world
- Valerie Draves, who is a catalyst to pull together a gathering of transformative souls
- Violet Igonikov, who is a flame of truth and wisdom, fueled by faith.

On our first call, we had a group meditation. We walked through a forest until we got to a ledge overlooking a great valley, surrounded by mountain peaks. We walked down to the center of the valley and there held hands in a circle. As we watched, a vortex of molten gold formed in the center of our circle. We stood around this vortex for some time, just soaking in the incredible energy. And as we did so, we saw people streaming in between the mountains, coming to the valley, drawn to us and the energy we were producing.

We began to call ourselves the Galactic Sisterhood, in recognition of a sense that we were a council formed from different galaxies, called together here in this time and space.

Now, I need to mention here that I am not completely comfortable with this idea. I am not a person who gives much thought to aliens, galaxies, ancient civilizations or the like, and a part of me would really prefer to keep it that way. Frankly, it just seems a little weird to me.

But I have to remember that I once felt that way about the intuitive senses; you may recall that I hid the *You Are Psychic* book under 'normal' books at the checkout stand. And I have also promised to tell you about my actual personal experiences. So in fairness, I should relate two experiences that actually give credence to the galaxy quest idea.

During one of our calls, we stood again in our circle holding hands, with our backs to the glowing vortex. I saw distant galaxies pouring energy into our eyes, each of us receiving energy from a different galaxy. And it felt powerful. It felt true.

My second experience was during our call on the night of the Winter Solstice, 2008. As we stood in our circle around the vortex, I suddenly became aware that we were surrounded by some sort of beings. I say 'beings' because they were definitely not people, angels or anything recognizable to me. They were also not like anything I have ever seen portrayed in the movies.

I can still clearly recall the image of these beings, glowing in the darkness around us, floating in the air. I looked closely at one, in particular. His head was made of gold light and was formed in a triangular wedge. It was difficult to see in the darkness, but beneath that wedge, where a body would be, it looked like a very, very long robe, just draping down shapelessly.

These beings were not frightening at all; in fact, the feeling coming off of them was quite neutral. I understood that they were there to lift us to a higher energetic state.

I felt them lift us and then I saw us dissolve into atoms that looked like little stars, so that we were a circle of stars, like the thick part of the Milky Way. And I had the sense that when we reformed we would be different than we were before the experience.

I should make one last comment. The others at this meditation did not see what I saw. We were each having a different experience. So perhaps it was just a mental metaphor of energy that my mind created. Or perhaps—could it be?—they were visitors from my galaxy and I was the only one who could see them. Hmmm...

I continue to be in contact with some, but not all, of the Galactic Sisterhood. Perhaps this time of joining and increasing our energies was, in fact, the purpose of our meeting. As I've learned from the soul landscapes, it is not always necessary to do things together in the physical world in order to accomplish a mission.

<u>Courage of the Creative Spirit</u>

Doreen and Nancy, two of the Galactic Sisterhood members, told me of Coco Fossland, who coaches people in turning their passion into a profitable business. In December of 2008, Coco was doing a free 7-day manifestation journey. I decided to participate.

126

Every day, for 7 days, we were to do one of her guided meditations and then follow through on various assignments, all of which were to lead to manifesting something that we were passionately excited about creating. I decided to focus on my one-woman show, *Courage of the Creative Spirit*.

This is a show I had written a couple of years before. In the few performances I gave, I had received a wonderful response. I was thinking about how to market it, perhaps by seeking corporate sponsorship. At the time, I had one booking for the show, planned for February.

First, let me tell you a little about the show. I tell the inspiring stories of the greats of musical theater, including these: how Oscar Hammerstein wrote flops for ten long years before he finally teamed up with Richard Rodgers to write *Oklahoma!*; how Rodgers himself came within one day of becoming a baby clothes salesman instead of a composer; and how Alan Jay Lerner had to see a psychiatrist before he could finish writing *My Fair Lady*. And of course, I follow each story with one of their songs, giving me the opportunity to sing some of the greatest songs ever written.

Coco began the 7 days with an interesting meditation. We were to ask a manifestation mentor to come to us, to give us guidance for the 7-day journey. We were to choose someone, real or imaginary, personally known to us or not, who had successfully done what we wanted to do and had sustained it for a period of time. I selected Barbra Streisand as my manifestation mentor.

Ms. Streisand was kind enough to show up during my meditation and to accept her role. But her advice was not about marketing. She told me to lift my level, to own the stage, to be a star! She told me to improve the show as well as my performance, to make every moment flat-out fabulous.

The show was my primary focus from late December, 2008, until the scheduled performance in late February, 2009. I added a new opening number and strengthened a few weak parts in the narrative. I practiced over and over. I developed a pre-show routine to pull the energy of the Galactic Sisterhood vortex into my body as I pictured myself performing at the Hollywood Bowl. I held rehearsals for my friends in my living room. I lost another 5 pounds. The show got better and better and so did I. I invited everyone I could think of to attend.

At various times I wanted to quit, but then I would practice my show one more time and hear myself telling the stories of these great songwriters, stories which were all about not giving up, believing in yourself, and continuing on no matter what.

Finally, the day of the performance arrived. I peeked out and saw my little granddaughters in the front row. I pulled the energy of the vortex into myself as I pictured myself on the stage at the Hollywood Bowl. Then I stepped out onto the stage and gave the best performance of my lifetime. The audience was attentive and delighted. My voice never sounded better and I truly owned the stage — Ms. Streisand would have been proud!

Twinkle of an Eye

Coco then asked if I wanted to sign up for a year of paid coaching. I asked Quado. He said yes. I asked other friends who were in touch with spirit. They got 'yes'. I asked Quado again and he said: "Are you going to keep asking until someone says no? The answer is yes!" So I signed up.

From Coco, I learned about the Authentic Customer. The concept behind the Authentic Customer is that there is a person whom you are meant to serve, someone who needs and wants what you have to offer—and who will actually pay you for your product or services, if you meet his or her needs. The exercise is in the form of a meditation, so that you will use your spirit to access this truth.

In the Authentic Customer meditation, I entered a clearing in a forest, where a table for two was set. My Authentic Customer entered the clearing; she said her name was Naomi. Naomi said that although she has done everything right, married a good man who provides well for the family, had great children who do well in school, had taken care of herself physically, she feels her life has no meaning. She feels listless and adrift, wondering why she is here. She said she wants to spend three days with me to be utterly transformed into a person who wakes up in the morning full of energy and enthusiasm for life.

My first thought was that this three-day retreat needed to happen in Maui, at the Hotel Hana Maui where I had stayed during my Karuna Reiki classes and where I had my Jesus visions. My next thought was that I would need some help to pull this off in three days!

I immediately thought of Valerie and Bernadette, two members of the Galactic Sisterhood whose transformational power was so strong that my voice got loud when I was describing their soul landscapes. I sent emails to both of them, asking them if they would like to put on a retreat in Maui with me.

By now, Valerie and I had become close friends. We both live in Southern California and the first time I met her in person, I invited her to Thanksgiving dinner! Naturally, she fit in with my friends and family perfectly, as if she had known us all for years. She also came to my show rehearsals and to the show itself, something that got her a lot of points in my book.

Valerie contacted me right away when she received my email and we began working out what we could do for Naomi, our Authentic Customer. Valerie told me she had always loved the idea of instant transmutation, in the twinkle of an eye. I immediately thought of the wonderful recitative in Handel's Messiah: "And we shall all be changed, in a moment, in the twinkling of an eye. "

Valerie and I continued to develop the concept of Twinkle of an Eye and our fabulous retreat at the Hotel Hana Maui, with peaceful cottages overlooking the surf, no telephones, no television, just peace and beauty. A perfect spot for transformation!

But where was Bernadette? I sent another email. Days passed. Still no word.

Finally, one morning I got an email from Bernadette. I read it and after I picked my jaw up off the floor, I immediately called Valerie: "You won't believe this!"

It turned out that Bernadette hadn't responded because she was on vacation with her grandchildren. Where? In Maui. But not just any place in Maui. Right at that moment she was writing her email from the very hotel where Valerie and I had been planning the retreat, the Hotel Hana Maui, on the remote end of Maui, definitely off the beaten path.

Bernadette had planned to go camping, but the campground was closed so they traveled on to Hana. There she saw the beautiful lava cross on the hill and a lovely hotel. Something told her that she should stay there, if only for one night. She got a room, then went to the hotel business center to see if there were any urgent emails.

And there she was now, in the very hotel we had written her about, reading our email.

But Bernadette and I were no strangers to serendipity. Before signing up for my Soul Session, she had seen a vision of a red-headed woman and had understood that she was to work with her. One day she happened upon my website and there I was—the woman she had seen in her vision. She had signed up for my Soul Session, during which I had seen her awesome power.

And now she had "accidentally" gone to the very hotel I was writing her about. Was this a message that the three of us should begin to work together? Well, yes!

So, Valerie, Bernadette and I built our website, www.TwinkleofanEye.com, to offer our Maui retreat. For many weeks, we met weekly to explore and expand upon the awesome power that happens when then three of us focus together. We laughed as we shared life experiences. We explored and expanded our individual and joint powers. And, importantly, we allowed ourselves to be three women who are great, shining and powerful, and who can say it aloud.

Power Animal Adventures

After a time, Valerie and I decided to conduct Adventures on www.PowerAnimalsUnleashed.com, the site I had created from my shaman experience. We called them Adventures, because we truly had no idea what would happen—and Valerie and I do love the fun of not knowing! We took a group of people with us in a meditation, an hour or two in which we simply described what we saw as we explored the world of spirit.

We had a weekly adventure for a period of ten weeks. Each adventure built on the one previous, teaching us amazing lessons about the earth, about people, about serendipity and spirit. During these sessions, we met the Ancient One, a giant sperm whale who is as old as the earth herself. We met the Man from Ur, the original man, who inspired me to make a movie honoring the earth and her animals (see the movie on www.PowerAnimalsUnleashed.com). We made two great new friends, Beverly from Canada and Sally from Australia, who joined us on each and every adventure. We expanded and expanded, our energies growing wider and deeper each week.

And then one day it was done. The last session was two hours long and it summed up everything we had learned. And we knew that this experience was over and that we had been transformed by it, just as we had been transformed by the energies of the Galactic Sisterhood and the Power of Three we discovered in Twinkle of an Eye.

There was a very important lesson to be learned from the experiences of this year. I plunged into each experience with enthusiasm and energy, giving it everything I had. I built websites and created movies and videos. I thought, because I felt so strongly that each step was what I was meant to do, that perhaps in each case I was about to launch into a new career. I thought, "Ah, this is it! This is what I am meant to do!"

Yet each one of the experiences reached a time when it felt complete, that it had done its job, that I had taken from it what I needed. And it was necessary then to let it go.

At first this was confusing and disappointing, since I had invested so much time and energy in each step. But after a time, I began to understand that this is the way the adventure unfolds. Each step was, in fact, what I was "meant to do" at the time. I was simply not meant to stop, build a business and stay within any of these steps. I was meant to keep moving into new energies, mysteries and adventures of the spirit.

And the most mysterious of all is the last adventure of this most amazing year, the discovery of 17-21-35.

17 − 21 − 35

I thought that I had completed this book, that I had said all I had to say. But somehow it didn't feel quite complete, so I set it aside to wait. And now I see that it was waiting for me to have yet one more experience to relate.

A New Adventure

When our weekly Power Animal Adventures completed their cycle, I felt that I needed to shift my focus to my consulting business for a time, where I was becoming very busy. And yet, Valerie and I also began to sense that we had an assignment, some additional energy work we needed to do.

Valerie kindly offered to take the lead on our behalf, since she had more available time: she would work consciously and I could participate super-consciously, while focusing my time on my consulting.

It was not clear to us what this energy work was, just that Valerie was to meditate as much as possible. As the days moved forward, we noted that we had frequent headaches, something unusual for both of us. We also felt the need to rest often. If I even walked by a couch, my body just yearned to lie down, if only for a moment.

One day, Valerie and I were discussing some of what she had been experiencing in her meditations. We went deep together to see if we could interpret the symbolism. Then we saw the number 17 and understood that we were to build a bridge to link our physical world to this unknown place we associated with the number 17.   We then saw the number 21 hovering in the air further off and the number 35, even further than that.

I need to make an aside here about terminology. We experimented with using different words to refer to these places of mystery. Dimension 17. Area 21. But in the end, these words carried too much weight from things that had nothing to do with what we were experiencing here and now. So finally we found ourselves just using the numbers. And that felt exactly right.

When we first noticed 21, we both saw spiked heels (I saw Manolo Blahniks and she saw Jimmy Choos) and red-carpet gowns, of all things.   I remember that we laughed and remarked that apparently we would be required to dress up in order to go to 21. But first we had a bridge to build, the bridge to 17.

We had the strong sense that this bridge was urgently needed. This sense of urgency was very unusual, for the world of spirit is timeless and eternal. But the urgency was real and tangible and all the more significant for it being outside our normal experience. We also felt that everything else we had done, the entire spiritual journey we had each taken over the last 15 years, had been in preparation for this, the building of this bridge. It also seemed that everything in this extraordinary year had been leading us step by step to this moment, when we would be ready to undertake this urgent and incredibly important job.

And what, exactly were we to do to accomplish this urgent task? Just continue, headaches, fatigue and all. Continue meditating and allowing the mystery to unfold in its own way. And why were we the right people to do this? Because we embrace mystery and gladly do what we cannot fully understand and explain. In fact, we love it dearly.

I also suspect that many others have been working alongside us. It is my hope that this book may bring forward some of the others who have also been making their way to 17-21-35.

Our Great Achievement

And one day, on July 24, 2009, Valerie awoke to the sound of applause. She called up to ask me if I knew why she felt surrounded by joy, laughter and loud applause. I responded that I didn't really know, but that I had been seeing a glowing white bridge with a lot of scaffolding underneath it. The minute the words were out of my mouth, we knew. They were all clapping because we had done it, we had finished the bridge to 17!

We took a few minutes to marvel at the bridge. As we watched, white angels took their places along the bridge, and there they have remained. Our vision of the bridge since has flashed back and forth between a suspension bridge and one with scaffolding underneath, but the white glow and the angels are constant.

We had once thought that the purpose of the bridge might be to allow 17 to come to our world, but no. It was clearly a one-way bridge from here to 17.

We stepped onto the bridge and walked across. At the end of the bridge was a portal of concentric circles, expanding out from the center, like a pebble tossed into a pond, over and over. We took a deep breath and stepped through to 17.

Once in 17, all emotion just disappeared. We found ourselves in a place of absolute objectivity. Everything in 17 feels clean and neutral. Nothing is good and nothing is bad. Everything simply is. And 17 is elastic; there is room for everything here.

We saw narrow vertical stripes of colored light and had a sense that these stripes held intelligence. The colors were not within the color spectrum we know. We each turned sideways and slipped into a stripe. Once in, we realized that each stripe was endless, that it went up and down to infinity.

We also felt that 17 is a place of instant shared knowledge of what is. Before we entered 17, we were not within What Is 17. Once we entered, What Is 17 simply included us; when we left it would not. And there was no emotion or judgment about whether we were a part of What Is 17 or not.

It appears that 17 is a place where we are cleansed of emotions, attachments and expectations, of everything that is not simply What Is. We began to see that 17 is a way station to prepare for 21.

We saw a dressing room and knew that we were to get dressed to go to 21, just as we had first sensed. We put on fabulous gowns and ridiculously high heels and swept up our hair. My gown was green silk and it flared out when I twirled; my shoes were strappy and silver. Valerie was a vision in scarlet; her shoes were made of sparkling colored light. We were gorgeous!

When we emerged from the dressing room, two men awaited us, our escorts. They were in tuxedos, tails, and were beyond handsome, even down to a Cary Grant cleft chin. They held out their arms for us to take and walked us across a red carpet that had appeared, toward a curtain at the end. The curtain drew back and we stepped into 21.

I could not believe my eyes. There it was, that same stage I had been seeing in visions, outdoors like the Hollywood Bowl, with an audience of thousands. But this was not an audience of people; it was an audience of light, thousands of sparks of light.

We were flooded with the most intense joy. We danced and danced, our gowns flowing, our handsome escorts leading us lightly, trippingly, across the polished wooden stage. There was no music playing; the music for the dance came from within.

And then we knew where we were. 21 is the Dream Come True place. It is the Answered Prayers place. It is the place where our earth dreams become reality.

I looked down and saw that I was made up of particles of light. I changed quickly to a tiger and back again; I could become anything at will. Valerie said she could see through herself, because she was made of light and only light. Anything is possible here—and it is all accomplished by changing our own form. That is the power we are given in 21, to change ourselves, thus changing everything.

Then we saw that there was an arcing light from 21 to earth. We saw the cycle of light and energy as it crossed the bridge from earth to 17, then into 21, then arced back to earth. And then the cycle moved faster and faster, earth-17-21-earth, until it was vibrating in every cell of our bodies and formed a cloud of energy around each of us.

We could also see 35 looming out in the distance, but for now, this was quite enough, thank you!

The Yellow Brick Road

A week or so later, I called Valerie from the freeway. I had a sense that we had something we needed to do. I could see that there was fog and mist covering the forest near the Bridge to 17, and that people were not able to find it. As we talked, I realized that we were to build a yellow brick road leading to the bridge, right then, as I drove the freeway to downtown Los Angeles. (Don't try this at home.)

First we saw the stacks of bricks. Then, suddenly, the road was built, just like that. As in the Wizard of Oz, it was sparkling and golden and went on for miles and miles, through the misty forest and the valleys beyond, running through deep mountain passes and across open meadows of daffodils, for mile after mile. We realized that the road was so long because it is there for everyone who seeks it, no matter where you are. Even if you are in the fog and darkness, you will be able to see it, to feel its energy coming up through your bare feet, guiding you along to the Bridge to 17 and then to 21.

I mentioned something to Valerie about 35 and I heard, "You can go there now, if you wish." We can? Yes, yes, we're ready! So we ran across the bridge and into 17 and went straight to the dressing room. We still put on gowns and heels, but this time we felt we should leave our hair down, long and wavy. We looked like those models with fans blowing their fabulous tresses back, as we took the arms of our handsome escorts and moved gracefully into 21.

I had assumed we would again be dancing, but instead we left our escorts below as we instantly started to fly—no wonder we left our hair down! We flew up and up toward 35, lifting effortlessly.

And now I must apologize, for it is my task to try to find words to describe 35 and it cannot be done. 35 is a place of pure spirit, wide open and expansive, endless, infinite. We could feel the presence of so many, all delighted to have us there. Valerie said she felt "immersed in presence." But at first, there was nothing to see, just a feeling of oneness, of love, of grace and gratitude. Let your mind reach back to a moment of deep beauty and connection, perhaps when you watched gulls flying over the ocean or first glimpsed a snow-capped mountain. Go deep into that feeling and then multiply it many times over. That is 35.

Then we saw Jesus with arms outstretched, with an enormous embrace to encompass us. We went toward him and into him. It was as if we were stepping into a hologram of his energy; we felt and knew him as a vast energy field we could enter and become one with. We stayed in this infinite grace and love for a time.

We saw that there was a radiant light shining down from 35 to 21, like a movie projector. And we understood that while 21 is the place of glorious earthly manifestation, the place where you live the life you desire, 35 is even more. 35 is the place from which 21 is projected. 35 is the place where the movie is made and 21 is merely the projection of it. And then we heard, "Work from here."

Ah, yes, of course, work from here. Lift up into this, be within this, be this. I am this. You are this. We are this. Work from here.

By the way, not surprisingly, I missed my offramp, got totally lost and was late to my meeting.

And Now...

And now the mystery truly begins, for we do not know what comes next. We know that we are to learn to live simultaneously on the earth and in 35. We believe that if we lift up into 35 consciously as often as possible for a while, that this will become a natural part of how we live our daily lives.

I feel things begin to shift within me, now that I am consciously in touch with 35. What I feel now is that the struggle is finally over, that the battle of me against myself seems to be winding down, as my body and mind begin to calm. I no longer feel the need to condition my mind against negative thinking or to use will power to struggle against physical cravings. All of that seems to be gradually and unexpectedly subsiding. And the irony of it is this: even as I am beginning to effortlessly achieve what I have so long struggled for, it no longer seems important. Fat or skinny, negative or positive, rich or poor, young or old, I am still "that," the essence of me within 35.

A mantra came to me that seems to take me to 35 very easily, especially if I chant it. Chanting it in the shower in the morning seems to be particularly effective. It is:
"Ohn-tah ah oom" or "ohn-tah ahm oo." The placement of the 'm' doesn't seem to be important; what matters is the flow through the vowel sounds, oh, ah and oo. And if it naturally evolves into something else as you chant it, that is fine, too.

A Great Little Story
I do have a fun Post-35 story to tell. I was at a client, sitting under a loudly buzzing light, getting ready for a presentation. The little blue lights on my laptop were flickering, but my screen suddenly went completely blank. I tried everything: rebooting, walking away, poking at all the keys, giving it Reiki. Then I thought, why am I pushing so hard? Perhaps this is just how it should be. So I relaxed, lifted into 35, saw the cosmic projector and felt the rush. (Did I mention the rush? It's like a flood of grace that comes over me when I enter 35.)

I asked my favorite question: "How shall I deal with this?" The answer came immediately: "Turn the computer off and let it be. There is a lot of electrical interference." So that's just what I did. I turned it off, relaxed and just sat there being peaceful, with no expectations whatsoever.

After a few minutes, the voice in my head spoke again: "OK, try it now." So I turned the computer on and voilá, it worked!

New Thinking

Certain things seem like old thinking in the post-35 world. For example, the spiritual concept of surrendering to God or my higher self no longer feels quite right. Instead, it feels as if I am to seek harmony with myself, harmony with a feeling of oneness that is within 35 that is within me that is me. What I find myself doing is a little like surrendering, in that I am pulled into a state of complete acceptance of what is, but the power is still, somehow, all within me.

The other day, Valerie said perhaps our souls had made an agreement to do all this during our lifetimes, and we both suddenly said, "No, no, old thinking!" It doesn't feel as if there is any prearrangement, any plan, any rules. It feels more lively and spontaneous than that. It is as if my soul, or higher self, or whatever that essence of me is that I found in 35, is just looking around, having fun and enjoying the experience of it all, and then suddenly says, "Oh, I think I'll do that!" And Valerie's soul says, "Oh, how fun, I think I'll do that too!" And then Valerie and I, down here in this physical life, both feel compelled to do something and we just know that our greatest personal harmony lies in following that feeling.

And so we do. We build a bridge and then a yellow brick road to reach it. And that, then, is what I now believe this book is, a guide along the golden, shining road that eventually leads to 17 – 21 – 35. I look forward to meeting you there.

By the way, Valerie saw a 99 glimmering off in the distance. I wonder when we'll be invited there. We can hardly wait!

ACCESSING YOUR GREATNESS

I know, absolutely, that you have within you, right now, exactly as you are, the seeds of true greatness. You are like every other person I worked with, with a soul of beauty, love and greatness, and with the power to truly transform the world.

This book is a call for you to step into that greatness, your own greatness, to let yourself shine out with all the light that is in you, illuminating not only your own life with joy and love, but that of those around you.

This book is a call for you to be the love that lives within you. It is a call not only for you to go far beyond the definition of success you were taught, but to go into the deep core of love and light that you truly are, to become the full expression of your life's highest purpose, of your soul's deepest passion and intention.

For I know this about you:

- I know that you are deeply and infinitely creative, fully capable of creating a life of joy, peace and love
- I know that you are deeply loving, that you are connected to everyone you know and have ever known in love and light
- I know that you are deeply and unconditionally loved, exactly as you are, right now, no matter who you are, no matter what you have done or left undone
- I know that you are surrounded by help and guidance at every turn
- I know that you are an expression of a higher spiritual being, a being of love and light that shines brightly within you, right now
- I know you are capable of lifting yourself up into this true light so that it fills you and illuminates you, so that you are a beacon lighting not only your own way, but that of others as well.

I know all of this about you absolutely, without any doubt. And the call I am issuing is for you to step into that infinite possibility that you are, to expand yourself up into the light that you are and to open your heart so that the endless stream of universal love runs through it every second of every day.

I know that the energy, love and light that you then generate are enough to light up the lives of thousands of people around you and that if only enough people learn to shine out with all that they are, the light will be so bright that the shadows of fear, ignorance, doubt and hatred will have no choice but to retreat and eventually disappear. And I know that you have this power within you.

Not only do you owe it to yourself to live a life of beauty, joy and love, but you owe it to the rest of humanity to shine out as brightly as you can, right now, in this very moment and in all of the moments of your wondrous life. The world needs your light and I know that it dwells within you.

If there is one message I wish to convey more than any other, it is this: the transformation of the earth and everyone upon it, from fear, anger and violence into love, peace and joy, begins inside each individual person. What is inside your heart, what you feel, is tangible and real and it floats out into the world, influencing not only your life, but that of everyone around you.

Your love, for yourself, your life and for others, opens up worlds of wonder around you, space in which others are allowed to be loving. Your inner peace creates a peaceful world in which others can find themselves, going beneath the loud voices of fear and into the quiet whisper of their own beautiful soul. Your joy and creativity, and your openness and courage in expressing it, allow everyone around you to express their own.

If you were to allow me to develop a Call to Greatness program for you — and I'm not at all sure that you should! — it would be this:

1. Learn to love not knowing. Begin to get used to the feel of mystery and to welcome it into your life. Do what feels right without knowing

why. And when things mysteriously end, let go without knowing why.

2. Begin your morning practice, no matter what. Go beyond excuses and find a way to carve out at least 30 minutes for yourself every morning. Look at the "Your Morning Time" chapter again for suggestions, but do what feels right for you. The main thing is this: do it unfailingly, as the most important thing in your life, the one inviolable space in every day, no matter what.

3. If you have not yet developed your intuitive senses, begin now, right now. It is so much fun and it will transform your life in so many ways, spiritually as well as in very practical ways, helping you in your career, your finances and all of your relationships.

4. In part of your morning practice, begin meditating in some form. Remember that many of the missions from the souls revolve around actions that happen only in meditative space. While you meditate, you may well be fulfilling the greatest mission of your life. And if not, you are definitely creating a portal through which miracles can enter.

5. Consciously change your thinking and speaking, pulling your mind out of the past and future and into this moment, over and over, every moment. Move it out of criticism and into love and wonder. Change your language, so that you speak only of this moment and the actions you are taking toward your dreams.

6. Every morning, at the end of your practice, breathe and ask: "How shall I focus my day?" Before every important decision or meeting, go deep and ask: "How shall I handle this situation/person?" Verify that the answer you receive feels right in your center. Then take a deep breath and just do it.

7. Move into courageous action. Learn to love the feeling of scary-good, where you are being challenged to do things that have always scared you, but feel right underneath, things that lead you into new ways of being, acting and relating. Seek a deep feeling of peace and calm in your center, even when the adrenalin is rushing through your body.

8. Move into deep integrity with yourself. Learn how your body feels when you are acting on your own personal truth. Learn to follow that truth when you speak and act. Allow yourself to know what it is like to shine out in your own very personal, individual way. Be who you are!

9. Note to Do-ers: Get a move on! Get ready for your dreams to be realized. Practice that piano, record that demo, do those exercises, study that language, if only for 15 minutes every day. Put yourself into a state of complete readiness, so that the angels will know exactly who to bring into your life.

10. Note to Be-ers: Don't let the Do-ers push you around! If setting goals doesn't feel right, then stop trying. So many of my clients were relieved to hear me say what they already

knew: they are meant to be, not to do. Do-ers just love to set goals and deadlines. If you are a Be-er, they are a painful distraction.

11. Reach out in community to like-minded people. Remember that many of the soul missions involve locating and connecting with your soul mates, on both the meditative and physical levels.

12. Feel your greatness and power expanding within you. Develop techniques to consciously move yourself into full power, if it is opening the top of your head to invite your soul self flow to down into you, or talking to Quado, or getting a power animal from PowerAnimalsUnleashed.com. Whatever it is, practice it in calm moments so it is there for you when you need it.

In sum: develop your intuitive senses, meditate and then move out into the world, courageously expressing your truth. Take full responsibility for your life from this moment forward. Own who you are, how you think, how you feel and all that you do.

Realize that you are spreading the energy of your emotions out to others, affecting the world around you every moment. Be the change you wish to see in the world; be it now. Shine!

APPENDIX

THE SOUL SESSION
TRANSCRIPTS

I conducted over 80 soul sessions before I felt that the experience was complete; this appendix contains a representative sampling. Some share patterns with others I encountered; some are completely unique in my experience. But each is presented here as an individual, not formed into composites. (I have allowed each client to decide whether to use their name or a pseudonym.)

As you read these soul journeys, I invite you to move into the energy of the soul being described and see where you resonate. The purpose here is not to categorize yourself, for you are unlike any other. The purpose is to let your soul sing out when it will, thereby guiding you to a deeper knowledge of who you are and what you are here to do.

Just relax, breathe, and invite your soul self to join you in this journey. Take your time. Stop and contemplate when you care to. Make a little check mark in the margin if you suddenly get chills and recognize yourself.

∞

Patty

Patty is a legal secretary who is interested in helping women find a voice.

As we did her energy clearing, we found that her heart was her strength. Her heart is very open and vulnerable, but the vulnerability is itself the strength, for it allows her to remain wide open to the ever-flowing, ever-strengthening river of universal love.

She can also use the love in her heart to clear her center of old emotions, so that her center is now a clear pool of peace. Then she can look deeply into this pool and slide down the pool to the mansion of her soul, lying right there in her center.

Patty can walk through the hallways of this great mansion and open the door she feels drawn to, one door for each meditative experience. She will then walk through the doorway and into another life of her soul self. And she will find all of the love and all of the wisdom of that lifetime contained in the room, the room that was filled when that lifetime transitioned back to the soul. And when Patty's life is over and she transitions, her love and experience will fill one of these rooms in her soul's mansion.

Then we lifted up into her soul space, and here we saw that it is full of light, strands and streaks of colorful light, and all of this light is love, love from all of the lifetimes, love swirling and moving about. In

155

the soul landscape, all of the love is vibrant, glowing and moving, but her soul has poured it down into Patty's center, into the mansion of rooms, to give it form, so that she might more easily access it.

Her souls' passion and delight is love, to learn forms of love, to experience love. And she wishes for each of the lives she spins out on strands of light to not only experience life and love intensely, but also to reach out to others, feel their hearts and their love, pull all that love in and make that other soul's love a part of the whole storehouse of love that circles within the lights that are this soul self.

And so Patty's mission is to keep the love open and flowing, to keep reaching out to others and opening to their love.

∞

Karen

Karen is in Public Relations in the entertainment industry, a highly appropriate profession for her unique gifts.

When we lifted up into her soul space, at first it seemed to be a barren desert. But then we discovered her special gift.

Karen can look out on the barren desert, with its dry cracked surface, and to her, it's full of seeds, buried under the cracked earth. And then, when she looks at a seed, she can see it fully realized. She can see the redwood here and the lily there, as they will be when they are watered and grow into their full selves.

And what is more, Karen is herself the waterfall; she has the ability to create, to birth, to give life, to that seed. She pours her waters on the seed and it grows.

Karen needs courage and tenacity, because she sees the seed germinating underneath the soil, but to others, she appears to be pouring her waters on a piece of barren earth. Finally, a little green shoot appears and others can see it as well, but not until then.

Karen would do well with a team to help nurture and protect, to treat the little green shoot properly. And she should give them strong guidance, because she is the only one who can see which little green shoot is a redwood and which one is a lily. And this would then free her to focus on her great gift: to locate and birth the seeds.

∞

Violet

Violet works in the financial sector and has a big dream, to bridge the gap between the spiritual and corporate worlds. She is particularly interested in working with and inspiring young women to step into their greatness.

Violet's throat energy, the energy of self-expression, is unusually open and expansive. Her center has a flame within it, a flame of truth and wisdom, fueled by faith. She has only begun to tap the wisdom that lies within her. The flame will leap higher and higher; the smoke will fill her. She has so much truth to share and a great drive to share it.

When we lifted up into her soul self, we saw bonfires, and each bonfires was a past life. These lifetimes spun out by her soul were all very curious and inquisitive; they were scholars and scientists and experimenters. Her soul's delight is in learning, but her soul's passion is to take all of this wisdom from the ages and share it, spread it, light up the world with it.

Violet is invited to become consciously one with her soul, to walk on a pathway through all of these bonfires and breathe in the wisdom and experience. There is also a pile of wood in her center, the fuel of faith, and she may use it to build the fires higher and higher.

All of the wisdom from all of the lives is accessible to Violet. She will start talking, thinking she knew what she would say, and find herself saying the most incredibly wise things, just pouring out of her intuitively. She will be able to access wisdom far beyond her years.

∞

Wanda

Wanda is a healer and it is clearly what she is meant to do and be.

When we lifted up into her soul, we found a vast jungle. As we walked through the jungle, we discovered that the other lives her soul had spun out

158

had been earth healers, shamans, medicine men, who knew the ways of the jungle. As each of these lives had transitioned back to the soul, they had buried a box containing everything they had learned, full of knowledge, symbols, potions and herbs.

Wanda may come here in her meditations and walk through the pathways in the jungle. When she happens to step upon one of these spots where a box is buried, all of the knowledge will be energetically and intuitively transferred to her, flowing up from her feet through her entire body, changing her vibration and filling her with the energy and knowledge of the previous life.

Then her soul space expanded out and we saw that her soul is also a part of a circle of souls with whom she can share, to expand the knowledge. She will take the knowledge already in her soul and work with her soul circle to take it even higher and deeper. And when Wanda's life on earth is complete and she transitions back to her soul, she will take everything she has learned, put it in a box and bury it in the jungle to be passed on to another life.

Wanda's soul's delight is to have her learn from the past lives and then combine it all in new ways, to help people within her own time and also to be able to increase the storehouse of knowledge for the next life.

She is to come up to her soul space in meditation and then study and experiment in her life. When she works with other healers, she should know that she is a peer, not an apprentice, for she has within her the capability to discover new ways of healing.

∞

Marisol

Marisol has two careers, in the military and as a consultant, She dreams of being in a wonderful marriage and raising a family.

When we lifted into Marisol's soul landscape, it instantly expanded outward to show us that her soul's passion is in connection with others. Her soul is a part of a vast soul circle, each a glowing golden ball hanging in space. And all of these souls have spun out lives like stars, tethered to her with beautiful strands of light. And all of the stars and all of the strands flow out and intertwine and intermingle, forming a beautiful network of souls and lives.

Her soul's delight is when one of her lives meets up with a soul mate who shares the same time and space.

Some of the soul mate relationships are short and some long, some deep and some not, but they are all important. It is important to connect when they appear, but also important to let them go when their time is up, to learn to let it all be as it is meant to be and not chase after what has ended.

Inside Marisol, in her center, is a symbol and a signal, and these are meant to be broadcast in order to pull her soul mates toward her. This is how they will recognize each other, by the symbol and the signal they are meant to broadcast. But in order to broadcast, Marisol needs to keep herself clear of fear and doubt and past emotions, because the symbol and signal in her center must pass up through a clear space and into her heart, and her heart must be open so that the heart beat containing the symbol and signal can go out into the world and attract those it is meant to attract.

∞

Kae

Kae has glaucoma and has dedicated her life to the cause of bringing free eye care to the children of Nepal. In her energy clearing, I found her heart to be enormously strong. We saw it as a fountain of love, pulling in from the universal flow of love, then just flowing up and out.

When we lifted up into her soul, it was bright and golden. And then we saw that her soul self is an enormous fountain of love. It pulls in love from the universe, compresses it and makes it more powerful, then sends it out in enormously high fountains of golden glowing, flowing love. The word 'power' kept repeating; her soul self is enormously powerful, and all of the power is based on love.

Then her soul expanded outward and we could see other souls, all beautiful, flowing fountains. Some were high and powerful, some lower and gentler.

Then her soul expanded farther and we saw the most amazing sight. We saw that there was a whole system of water souls. There were water souls gathering up the waters of love that flow through the universe and feeding them to the fountain souls, who then compress the waters with their power so that they become great fountains that send a spray of love out into the universe.

Kae is a lifetime spun out by one of the fountain souls and she has all of the power and strength that she needs to fulfill her mission. She is meant to be a mirror image of her soul in this lifetime, gathering the love that is flowing freely and pulling it together, compressing it to give it form, and then sending it out in a vast shower on those around her.

∞

Mireille

Mireille works in healthcare in Canada. She has been studying for years in the area of cognitive behavioral changes, especially with teenagers, and is about to open her new practice.

Mireille's Soul Session was unique and interesting in many ways, not least of which was the way her soul gave us tools that she might work with as we went through the energy clearing.

We went into her intuition through the expanding space between her eyes, and saw there a wide open galaxy, with a reach of knowledge and connection that was almost too vast to handle. But then we were given a great tool for accessing this incredible storehouse of information. Mireille is to set an intention, a focus, then go into her intuitive galaxy; she will see one star grow brighter. And this star will then begin to gather up all the information from the vast universe that applies to her intention, like concentric circles moving in to the star. The star will move closer and closer, and when it is right before her eyes in a blinding light, it contains all the focused intuition she will need.

In her mind space, we got another great and useful image. Her conscious mind with its busy, noisy thoughts, just curled up like a cat in the corner, quietly taking a nap.

Her heart has a great gift. It has strong muscular walls, so that she is able to open her heart completely to another, feeling what they feel, but yet not allow that energy to enter into the rest of her energetic system. Her heart connects completely, but yet keeps it contained. A great gift indeed for someone who works as a counselor!

Her center is full of a clear sparkling well of truth—and yet another tool. After Mireille finishes a session with someone, she can take her truth and use it to flush out her heart and re-strengthen her heart muscle. Then she can be completely healed and unharmed, no matter how intense the heart connection was. She should perform this as a ritual after each client session.

Up in her soul self was a forest of very tall trees, reaching up higher and higher until they touched the hem of God. Pouring down is deep knowledge, direct access to the deepest truth and wisdom.

The trees also contain knowledge from other lifetimes her soul has spun out. She may come here in her meditations, walk through the forest until she senses the right tree, then put both of her hands upon it and receive an intuitive download. She is not to try to grasp or understand anything at this time, just clear her mind, let it curl up like a cat, and receive the information.

The knowledge contained in all those trees is already within her, but the download is like adjusting the lens on a camera; what was somewhat blurry will be made clear and in focus, easily accessible.

We were about to return when her soul self stopped us, saying there was more to see. And then we expanded out into the soul circle, where her soul had arcs of light connecting to other souls.

Then we understood how these connections were related to the tree downloads and to her new practice. When she goes up into her forest and downloads from a tree, this triggers her intuitive marketing activity. The knowledge now within her activates the arc of energy to a soul mate, and the person who needs what she now has to offer will feel drawn to contact her.

∞

Marita

Marita is a Reiki healer by profession. Her Soul Session began like the others, with an energy cleanse from the head down. But when we reached her heart, her heart suddenly overflowed with love, love that then poured down her arms and into her hands. As we gazed at her hands full of love, Jesus appeared and took her hands in his—and then took over the entire session!

The session moved into an exploration of power, her power. We were led to understand that she is fully capable of developing her own methods of healing. The overall message from Jesus was simple and clear: I am within you, in your hands, and you have all the power that implies.

We had talked before the session about how she might need a technique to clear her energy of all she had picked up in healing sessions, perhaps to shield herself in some way. But instead, the reading was all about power, power so strong it burned off the residue, power and light so strong that nothing could cling to her. She definitely did not need shielding — she just needed to let herself shine out with her power.

Afterwards, Marita said that a clinic doctor had told her she was more powerful than she was letting herself be. Well, yes, I think so!

∞

Lynn

Lynn and I did a Soul Session together before I appeared on her radio show as a guest. She lives on Vancouver Island in a cottage on a 100-acre farm. Her dream is to have a syndicated call-in show.

Lynn's intuitive area was like an ocean, where sound and feelings were transmitted to her through the vast waters. Her heart had a strong protective muscle and a very special function. Lynn is meant to take her intuition in through her heart, to let the ocean pour in through her heart, where she sorts and filters it. She allows a lot of the information to simply flow through her heart harmlessly, but some of it she picks up and store in chambers in her heart.

This whole system needs to work together. Her intuition is so vast it would overwhelm her if it flowed directly to her mind. But through this strong and open heart, she can pick up the sorted information and funnel it up to her mind, to form the right words, that will then flow out through her mouth.

She needs courage to trust her heart, to trust that it is OK to open her heart fully and bring it all in, and then faith that she will find the right words to speak.

In her center, her truth is a very clear pool and the light shining within it is very strong. There is no doubt in her center. She knows her truth and the light from her center shines throughout her entire body. It would be difficult for her to live outside of integrity, very uncomfortable and would possibly make her ill.

The light in her center wants to expand and expand, glow out for the world. Right now it is like a flashlight seen down through a pool of clear water, but it wants to be a vast searchlight, a beacon shining out.

In Lynn's soul space, first we saw the galaxy she is a part of. There are streams of clear light coming in to her, but she then takes it inside and transforms it into colors of the rainbow. Inside her soul she is full of colored gemstones and crystals, all electric and passing the energy around, turning the stream of clear light into all the vibrant colors. No wonder she is in radio--she is, quite literally, a transformer!

∞

Nancy

Nancy is retired from her work with computers and is exploring entrepreneurial opportunities.

In her energy clearing, we found Nancy's throat to be open and expansive, but her heart is clearly her strength, with unbelievably strong river of love running thorough. And she can use that flow from her heart to keep her center clear.

In her center is a garden of past lives, each a flower, sending its perfume out into her intuition. And what is available to her in this garden is not only wisdom, it is heart. For each flower contains the heart and love of the life that was lived and this is the essence of its perfume.

When we lifted up, we found the sweetest soul, all full of flowers and sending out flowers. Her center was a mirror image of her beautiful soul.

Her soul creates lives as flowers and then exchanges love with the flowers it creates. The soul pours love into the lives, they then generate and experience even more love, and then send it back to the soul, where it is then expanded and poured back down, all in an endless cycle of creating more and more love.

Nancy's job is to be, not to do. She affects and transforms the lives of others simply by keeping herself clear and sending her perfume out into the world. She will not even know who is transformed, because she simply releases her perfume of love and energy into the world, where it rides on the breeze and falls down upon others. And the life it touches then has a little flower of love blooming in the heart, watered by a river of love flowing through.

Nancy is to learn to recognize and realize her vast power, power all driven by love. For we see in her soul a huge river of love flowing through, feeding all the flowers. And all of this power is in her. Nancy needs to know that her mere presence transforms people, freely given and floating on the air around her. Her only job is to keep clear and open to the flow of love, water her flowers and send out perfume.

∞

Steve

Steve is a truck driver who has meditated for many years. His wife died after a long illness and he now lives in a house in the country with two golden retrievers. He is finally feeling ready to reach out and connect again in love.

Steve's solar plexus is the center of his strength, where he has a very strong and secure sense of self. He needs to go here first, light his light, and then use that energy to then reach up and heal his heart.

When we lifted into his soul landscape, it immediately expanded out to show us an intimate circle of souls, who are his soul mates through the ages.   There are rainbow-colored flows of love moving among them. Each soul is like a golden ball of energy, shooting off sparks, which are their lives.

These souls are in each others' lives over and over, the same close circle, but in different roles. In one life, they may be short acquaintances and in other lives, in deep and lengthy relationships. But they meet again, over and over in lifetime after lifetime, playing different roles.

And this is the dance of his soul and the pleasure of his soul, to intertwine his life with that of his intimate soul circle.

∞

Valerie

You have met Valerie many times in this book. I first met her when she contacted me for a Soul Session, something she felt called to do one day. When I received her request for a Soul Session, I had a strong feeling about her, that we were somehow connected. When I finally met her in person, it was like meeting an old friend--and I'm delighted to say that's what we have become.

As I worked with Valerie in her Soul Session, my voice kept getting stronger and louder, because she is so full of power. Her soul is full of purpose and intention for what she wishes Valerie to accomplish during her lifetime.

What we saw was a gathering, a gathering of people who will combine their energies and transform the earth. Valerie is a catalyst to make this

169

happen, to pull together this gathering in the physical world. And she is fully empowered to accomplish this task.

I believe that our work together combines our two missions, but we shall see what life holds as we bravely venture out.

∞

Martha

Martha works as a caterer, but she has a dream of expanding on the energy/healing work she now does part-time.

Martha's intuition is vast and very, very strong. She was also very clear. But when we came to her center, an angel named Mary appeared. Mary wished to help Martha protect herself. She touched her wand to Martha's center, and Martha's whole torso became like a golden glowing ball, with a protective border.

Martha's challenge as a healer is to open her great intuition to connect to others, but yet protect herself from their pain. Mary said that she should call her before sessions to get protection and after each session for cleansing.

In her soul self, we saw that her choice to be a healer truly makes sense. Martha is a waterfall and a sun, helping others to flourish and blossom in whatever form they naturally grow, whether it is a redwood or a daisy.

She makes the soil fertile and sets the sun in the sky. She helps them be their best selves, whatever that may be. Her waterfall pours down into a pool that then spreads out and waters the world.

Her soul then expanded out to show us that it is also a part of a soul circle, a whole galaxy for Martha to connect to. After she learns better how to protect herself, she needs to actively reach out and make her soul connections.

∞

Kathy

Kathy is a Naturopathic doctor; she also does energy work. Connecting with Kathy was an amazing experience — she just about blew my circuits!

In our energy cleansing, her mind was like vast chamber. Her throat was like an unfolding rose in spring, just starting to learn how to express itself, but with a great desire to open into full blossom.

Kathy's center had no clouding from emotions, fear or doubt, just crystal clear access to her truth. It was also full of chambers from past lives, with their knowledge and experience all there and available to her intuitively. We could sense that some of the past lives were like shamans, very involved with plants and animals.

We lifted up to her soul self and had an amazing experience. At first, we saw the past lives standing around; they appeared to be people involved in nature healing. Then we began to see a vast network that connected knowledge from not only all the lives of her souls, but also from other souls to whom she is connected. And they were all

171

connected by great arcing lights, like electrical connections.

Her soul's passion is knowledge and connection, pulling in all of the experience from all of her lives and all of the lives of the souls in her circle, pulling it all in and letting it form new synapses. Great and beautiful patterns of light are formed as a new piece of knowledge sparks new connections. Her mind is endlessly connecting and reconnecting, in a great network, buzzing and snapping with electricity.

And it all combines, all of this experience, in completely original and unusual ways. The knowledge from a jungle shaman and the knowledge from a scientist in a laboratory are combined with the experience of a woman giving birth, and it all flows and feeds into Kathy's powerful computer of a brain, and new synapses form and endlessly re-form in more and more patterns of light and connection. Whew!

Kathy said that as a child she would get in trouble at school because she just knew the answers to math problems. She is one of those rare people who looks at a highly complex problem and says "The answer is 2."

Kathy's challenge is to realize that not everyone can do what she can do. She will do well to reach those other souls in her circle who are wired like she is, so she can spark off of them at a very high level.

∞

Patti

Patti is about to retire from her corporate career and move closer to her son and grandson.

In her energy clearing, we saw that her heart is her strength; she has a strong and open heart. Up in her soul landscape, her soul is a bright golden ball floating within a vast ocean of blue, along with other soul selves. They have spun out lives that are tethered to them and float in the beautiful blue ocean, calm and completely at peace. The lives spun out by all of the souls in the circle are intertwined; everything is connected by this ocean of intuition, love and spirit.

Her soul's delight is in this connection with other souls in her circle. And Patti has been gifted with a deep intuitive sense that she may use to make the connections and strengthen them.

Her soul's passion and purpose is effortless connection and being. Patti is to float and be. There is nothing she needs to accomplish. No goals she needs to set. Nothing but to be and to connect. And simply by being and deeply connecting with others, the spirit is made stronger and lifts all of them into greater and greater levels of spirit.

Peaceful, effortless and connected, with gold and blue light from her soul pouring down into her, filling her, calming her. This is Patti.

∞

Char

Char is a retired attorney, who once ran a high-powered private law practice. She and I have a number of parallels. When I was doing my own soul quest, I had a vision of myself holding up gems to the light; we saw this same vision within Char. She also shared that she has seen herself standing in front of an audience of thousands, just as I have.

When we lifted into Char's soul landscape, we saw that it was full of piles of gems. Her soul was part of a network of souls that all spin out gems, that are like stars in the galaxy, but are brightly colored jewels.

We had a sense that the gems represented the combining of beauty (art) and truth. Char has within her the capability for finding the truth and then expressing it beautifully. She is an artist, combining spirituality and truth with beautiful expression. She may find a calling in poetry or lyrics, but even more so with the visual arts, for she clearly has an eye. She may yet explore many means of artistic expression, eventually to find the right balance to bring out the truth and beauty that lie within her.

∞

Doreen

Doreen has a background in corporate management in the environmental field. She now does life coaching.

Doreen has also had the vision of being on a stage in front of thousands. And her soul landscape, while not exactly like Char's, also contains gemstones.

In Doreen's soul landscape, we saw gems as big as castles. There was one enormous castle the color of red garnet. We walked inside.

We found that the castles contain not only the wisdom from the other lives of her soul, but wisdom directly from God. The God light was streaming down into her soul directly, lighting up the castle from within

The delight of Doreen's soul is that she might find the right words to spread this great wisdom.

∞

Linda

Linda works in corporate management and is getting her PhD in organization and management, with an emphasis in leadership. She plans to do her dissertation on how spirituality affects leaders' ethics. Her grandchildren are her greatest joy.

Linda's energy clearing showed a very strong and heart and center, with a deep connection with her personal truth. It is understandable that she

175

sometimes struggles with the ethics within the corporate world, for her own personal truth is a driving force in her life.

When we lifted up into her soul self, we saw that her soul self creates lives like explosions of fireworks, spinning out into the world in beauty and light, propelled high into the night sky. Linda is one of these fireworks and she has a mission, to light up the darkness, to explode into that night sky over and over, shedding light in a great burst of energy.

Linda will need that strong heart and center for the courage and tenacity to keep doing this: to enter the darkness and to transform it with her powerful explosion of light. But the mission was clear and she has been given all the power, strength and energy she needs to accomplish it.

∞

Christine

Christine is a life coach. She has studied with an Indian guru for many years. Christine and I became friends over thirty years ago when we both worked together in computers.

Christine was perhaps the most quiet and peaceful soul I encountered. She is a very still grove of trees reaching up toward spirit; her soul is a vast forest of quiet and peace.

Christine's purpose is simply to be this, to reach her branches up higher and higher, to touch the hem of God.

If she cares to, Christine is invited to walk among the trees and learn from the wisdom of the ages. The trees have ring after ring of wisdom that she may access in her meditations. But really, it is not important for her to do so. And she does not have a purpose to consciously share what she learns.

Christine's energy flows out and affects others as a natural and effortless result of her inner peace. Her entire focus is on being, not on doing, and too much doing is a distraction from who she is meant to be, a grove of trees, silent and contained, her energy completely vertical and reaching into the heavens.

∞

Susan

Susan worked in the medical industry for many years. She is now searching for a new focus in her life.

We then lifted up into her soul space, which immediately expanded outward to show a vast circle of soul mates. And then the soul's purpose became very clear. The passion and intention of Susan's soul is to make deep contact with all of the souls in the circle — but at the soul level — and to vibrate together.

The souls within this circle share a vibrational frequency, a very high frequency. And when they vibrate together, it is multiplied thousands, millions, of times over. And when they are all connected and vibrate together, it will go out into the universe and transform and lift everything it touches.

But she cannot achieve this alone. She must team up with her soul circle.

Susan's mission is to locate as many of her soul mates as she can, regardless of what they are like in this life, and connect deeply with them at this higher level. And she is to do this by becoming a beacon, by going into a meditative state and learning how to vibrate at this high soul level. Then the others will be drawn to her.

Interestingly, what she and the others do in this lifetime, their careers and lifestyles, is totally irrelevant to accomplishing her soul's purpose.

∞

Ervene

Ervene is semi-retired; she does some work in Reiki and etheric body alignment. In the energy clearing, she was amazingly clear, with a strong heart and a deep and clear center of truth.

When we lifted up into her soul space, at first we could just see light-bodies moving around. Then we saw that her soul spirals up and up, higher and higher, until she dissolves into the oneness. And this is the delight and passion of her soul, to reach up into the oneness and be with it and within it, and then to spiral this energy down into Ervene.

There is a spiral of light running from the oneness, through her soul self and into her body. And it is a glowing white light, incandescent; it extends several feet out from her body, and as she builds it, it shines out for miles. There are other souls her soul is connected to that are like this, and we see them also as bright golden balls, but surrounded by a white light.

The light Ervene shines is transformative. She transforms the world around her simply by being and glowing and keeping her channel to her soul open. Ervene's mission is just to be and to shine; too much doing is a distraction.

∞

Alicia

Alicia has been working with mentally ill offenders for ten years. She would like to try new ways of counseling. She has studied shamanism and is about to study hypnotherapy.

In her intuitive space, Alicia has a very unique ability to focus. We saw a rose that started out as a bud; she focused upon it and it opened and blossomed, showing her its inner beauty and sending its perfume out into the world.

When we lifted up into her soul landscape, we saw a golden city. The walls were like ancient pueblo walls, but they were made of gleaming gold. As she approached a wall and touched it, the surface came to life and changed from being something inanimate to being something deeply alive, like a bear.

Alicia has a unique gift to bring people to life, to free them from their prisons. She also has the ability to see the gold where other people see a wall of mud.

Importantly, her way is unique. She has some very unique gifts that cannot be taught by anyone else. When she works with someone else, she needs to feel free to do it her way, no matter what they say. She is her own guru, the teacher who can show herself the way.

∞

Orlando

Orlando works in computers and lives with his family. In the energy clearing, when we reached his heart, it opened very wide, like it wanted to just keep expanding and filling with love.

When we lifted up into his soul space, we instantly saw that his soul is part of a circle of souls. We expanded out and it was as if we were in space, moving around the other souls like planets. All of the souls were connected by arcing strands of light and as we moved around, the strands intertwined.

Angels came and sang an ethereal song off in the distance, and all of the souls danced, making beautiful patterns of light. The main feeling was one of joy. Orlando's soul's passion is joy, joy through beauty, joy through music, opening to joy, creating joy, creating beauty.

Music should be a very clear path into joy, peace and love for Orlando. His opening heart should also open even wider through music. Dance, movement, beauty, joy, and music, these are the passions of Orlando's soul. He has a great capacity for joy.

∞

Carol

Carol is a singer, potter, and jewelry designer. She also does some esoteric healing, but she does not charge for it.

When we lifted up into Carol's soul, we immediately expanded out. It was like being in space, with planets and stars. We found that she has a special gift: to be able to lift up so high she is one with the mind of God. She has only to keep herself clear of old emotions, which can hold her earth-bound.

When Carol performs a healing, it is like opening a door to a stairway made of white light that she then climbs toward God. We then understood why she doesn't charge money for a healing session: she is getting as much out of each healing as she is giving.

∞

Cristina

Cristina has been both an educator and a dedicated mother. She has a dream to find a way to fold the holistic and spiritualistic into education.

Cristina's strength and center is in her mind. The moment I entered her mind, I felt the shadows of

181

ancient civilizations, like seeing the Parthenon in the background. We then discovered that her mind was full of rooms, endless rooms, and each contained the experience and learning of a lifetime. And all of her soul's lifetimes were focused on learning. This was her soul's passion, to learn, through intense involvement in life, through experimentation, as well as learning from others and from books. But always, always to learn. Her soul is hungry for knowledge and learning.

What was interesting here was that it was fine if she wanted to teach what she learned, but it was not necessary to fulfill her soul's intention. What was necessary was a deep and intense involvement in her life, so that she is creating another wondrous room in the vast mind of her soul. Learning alone is the purpose.

In her meditations, Cristina can walk down a long hallway and open the door to one of these amazing rooms of learning. With time, she will learn how to participate in the vivid learning experiences of her soul's other lifetimes and then fold that knowledge into her own vast and growing knowledge.

∞

Bernadette

Bernadette is a manager in a new-energy company. She also has a yoga/dance studio with her daughter. And, of course, she is my friend and partner in the Twinkle of an Eye adventure.

When I lifted into Bernadette's soul landscape, at first all I could see was a landscape of big boulders. As I approached a boulder, it suddenly appeared to be a castle, a dream castle. But then, when we walked inside the castle, we saw it was made of spirit. And this was the message from her soul self: that what appears to be solid and real is not; the truth is that everything is made of spirit.

Bernadette's role is to strip everything down to pure spirit and then rebuild, to manifest from pure spirit into new forms. And she has the great creative power to do this.

Then her soul expanded to reveal a circle of souls working together. They are all in the learning and growing phases of stripping away the boulders and castles; they are just coming to understand the depth of their creative and transformative power. As Bernadette does this herself, she will connect with these other souls to accomplish great things.

The power within Bernadette is awesome. My voice got loud when I spoke of it. She is full of creativity and power and the ability to manifest greatness and transformative forms.

∞

Sharie

Sharie is an accountant with a part-time healing practice. Her one really big dream is to be in a loving, healing relationship.

When we lifted up, we could see a white bird flying within the energy of her soul self. Her soul creates lives by setting them free, like soaring white birds, full of freedom and courage, free to create their lives in any way they choose, and given great gifts of talent and resourcefulness to do so.

Deep within Sharie's center are the birds of talent and creativity that she can set free. She must clear herself of the burdens of past emotion in order for them to fly. She has many talents she has not yet explored; she has within her the capacity for greatness.

Sharie will need discipline, patience and courage. She will free the birds who will soar on their wings of talent, creativity and greatness, but they will be buffeted by the winds of life, and she will need to build within her a safe haven, a tree where they can come and rest and be nurtured so that they can then fly free again.

And each time they go out in the winds and storms, they will grow stronger. Over time, they will begin to build her storehouse of wisdom and experience. And if she continues to nurture them and allow them to fly and grow stronger, always with patience and tenacity, some of them will break through the storm and reach up into the clear skies to fly in greatness.

∞

Kathleen

Kathleen lives on an alpaca farm in Australia. She also has a jewelry business, and this is her dream.

In her body clearing, the self-expression energy in her throat was very, very strong. It was like a great wind generated inside her and blowing out of her and into the world.

In her soul self, we learned that Kathleen has an enormously important task. Her soul is part of a vast soul galaxy and Kathleen's mission is to connect with the other people who are her soul mates, those other lives within this galaxy who share her time and space. When they connect, they will then form a grid of energy that will lift not only themselves but all of mankind to a higher energetic level.

During our session, it was emphasized that this was literal truth, and that over time she would come to truly own it and know that she has this awesome job before her.

We talked after the session about how she could use her intuition to create jewelry designs as signals to her soul mates. This would not only give her a means to reach her soul mates to accomplish her important assignment, but also would put her business into a very high energetic place.

We all wish Kathleen well on this awesome mission!

∞

Sabina

Sabina is deeply blessed with a beautiful, peaceful life with a much-loved husband on an island off Spain.

In our energy clearing, when we got to her heart, we saw that this is clearly her strength. An angel appeared, a beautiful angel with long, light brown hair, a white gown and wings, and a golden halo. For a time, the angel just watched the light and love swirling in Sabina's heart. Then she reached out her hand and, with Sabina's permission, touched her heart. As she did so, Sabina's heart expanded. It was like seeing space, but full of sparkling lights, all reaching out to spread love.

Sabina can use her strong heart energy to clear the rest of her body. She can go first to her heart, watch the light and love expand within it, and then let that light and love flow upwards to clear and quiet her mind, and down to clear her center.

Lifting up into her soul space, her soul felt very gentle and sweet, very soft, with a light touch. And as her soul self expanded out, it melded with a circle of souls. Then we saw that within each of the souls, in the center of each glowing golden ball of light, was a beating heart. These beating hearts pump out love, all beating in the same rhythm.

Sabina's soul has a great longing to join up with the other hearts who beat in the same rhythm, for when they do so, they create powerful waves of love that flow across the earth and out into the universe, transforming the world through love.

Sabina needs to make her choices all based on what comes from love and moves toward love. Her purpose is very simple, to live in love, to spread love, to be love, to reach out in love and to find the others who beat in the same rhythm, to form a community that loves, beats and creates love to transform the world.

About the Author

Carrie Hart: In Her Own Words

I wear so many hats. Sometimes it's fun and sometimes it's just crazy. But it seems to be who I am:

- A spiritual explorer, in the many ways touched upon in this book and undoubtedly many yet to come
- A management consultant
- A webmaster and Flash movie producer
- A singer/songwriter with two albums of original music and a third in progress
- A speaker/singer with a one-woman show, *The Courage of the Creative Spirit,* in which I tell the inspiring stories of the greats of musical theater and then sing their songs.

I live in the greater Los Angeles area with Ed, my terrific husband of over 35 years. We are fortunate enough to have children and grandchildren who live nearby. Ed and I also share our home with an embarrassing number of charming cats.

I have no set religious or spiritual beliefs. I just love that no one *really* knows what will happen next or why things happen as they do. I agree completely with Shakespeare's Hamlet, that there is more in heaven and on earth than is dreamt of in our philosophies.

If I could have my wish, everyone would greet the dawn with joy and anticipation, looking forward to a day full of mystery, laughter and fun, using their amazing intuitive and creative gifts in everything that they do. They would know, absolutely, that they are deeply loved and guided at every turn. They would shine out with their unique greatness as a natural part of who they are. I have done my best to capture this spirit in my book, *A Call to Greatness, the Exciting, Joyous Journey Your Soul Wants You to Take*.

Please visit me on my websites:
- CarrieHart.com is where you will find music and book downloads
- PowerAnimalsUnleashed.com is a very fun site that allows your intuition to select the perfect power animal for this moment in your life

- Quado.com has inspirational messages and meditations

- TwinkleofanEye.com invites you to a fabulous Maui retreat.

You may write me at carrie@carriehart.com. I would love to hear from you – especially if you have nice things to say about this book!

4377559

Made in the USA
Charleston, SC
11 January 2010